AN AMERICAN IDOL

Emerson and the "Jewish Idea"

Robert J. Loewenberg

UNIVERSITY
PRESS OF
AMERICA

LANHAM • NEW YORK • LONDON

Copyright © **1984** by

University Press of America,™ **Inc.**

4720 Boston Way
Lanham, MD 20706

3 Henrietta Street
London WC2E 8LU England

Library of Congress Cataloging in Publication Data

Loewenberg, Robert J., 1938–
    An American idol.

    Includes index.
    1. Emerson, Ralph Waldo, 1803–1882–Religion and
ethics. 2. Emerson, Ralph Waldo, 1803–1882– Influence.
3. Monotheism–Controversial literature. 4.
Liberalism–United States. 5. Antisemitism. I. Title. II.
Title: "Jewish idea".
PS1642.R4L6   1984   814'.3   84–7206
ISBN 0–8191–3955–6 (alk. paper)
ISBN 0–8191–3956–4 (pbk. : alk. paper)

All University Press of America books are produced on acid-free
paper which exceeds the minimum standards set by the National
Historical Publications and Records Commission.

For my mother

ACKNOWLEDGEMENTS

Chapters 1 and 2 are revised versions of an essay that first appeared in *The St. John's Review*, XXXIII (Winter 1982), 33–43, entitled "The Trivialization of the Holocaust as an Aspect of Modern Idolatry." Parts of Chapters 6,7 and 8 are revised versions of essays that appeared in *Center Journal*, 1 (Fall 1982), 71–100, and 2 (Summer 1983), 107–128 entitled respectively, "Freedom in the Context of American Historiography," and "Emerson and the Genius of American Liberalism." Chapters 3 and 4 are taken in part from an essay entitled "Emerson's Platonism and the 'terrific Jewish Idea,'" which appeared in *MOSAIC: A Journal for the Interdisciplinary Study of Literature*," XV (June 1982), 93–108.

CONTENTS

Preface

This book grew out of an attempt to provide to students, mostly Christians, some measure of self-understanding about the liberal civilization they have inherited. My purpose and theirs has been to uncover, in the context of American life and thought, the sources of liberalism's deadly hostility to the foundations of Western civilization, foundations which are also, of course, the sources of liberalism.

Naturally I cannot suppose that a book critical of liberalism, and especially of its greatest American patron and spokesman, Emerson, will be well received by academic intellectuals. Emerson is for literary intellectuals what Alexandre Kojève is for 20th century intellectuals simply, namely the "unknown Superior whose dogma is revered, often unawares." But if this small volume will be unwelcome among intellectuals, I look for a better reception elsewhere.

It is my hope that this book shall prove useful and also encouraging to students such as the ones I have had the good fortune to instruct at Arizona State University in the past decade and especially in the last five years. These students, I am sure, will find much that is familiar to them in the pages that follow. This, I know, will be the response of my friend and colleague Ben Sanders.

Sanders and his good wife Sarah Jane have prepared this manuscript for publication. Generous and devoted acts of this sort are common to this unusual young man. For this reason and others I am glad that I have this opportunity to record his great goodness to me. Ben Sanders, a rare distillation of the perfect student and scholar, though fond of noting how it was I who helped recharter the course of his life, has not fully appreciated how greatly he has affected mine. That wider audience due to his talents will await with eagerness, as I do, the appearance of his pioneering study of Nietzsche's Emersonianism.

I shall be quick to add that all errors in this book, large and small, are to be attributed solely to me.

Jerusalem 1984   RJL

CHAPTER 1

The Jewish Question in Contemporary Scholarship

If it is the case, as Yehuda Bauer has said, that "nothing has changed in the modern world about antisemitism but the language," then it is appropriate for scholarship, historical scholarship particularly, to consider this subject more seriously than it has done heretofore.[1] Certainly this is not to say that scholars have neglected the subject of the hatred of Judaism or the so-called Jewish Question in its many forms. Indeed one might even wish to argue that attention to this question from the standpoint of historical and ideological inquiry has been overdone. Rather it is to say that the question of Jewhatred has not been considered as a thing of transcendent, indeed of world-historical significance as it must be if nothing, in truth, has changed in the world "about antisemitism but the language."

There is of course a quite pertinent exception to the charge that antisemitism is not taken seriously by scholars. The enemies of Jewish things regard Judaism as transcending time and place. For example Marx and Hitler among moderns have looked upon Jewish subjects as deserving philosophic treatment. Typically, however, scholars have dismissed such efforts as rationalizations, preferring to treat would-be philosophic Jewhatred at the historical and phenomenological levels. In sum the treatment of the Jewish Question, of Jewhatred particularly, in its ideological and its existential aspects, betrays an unphilosophic approach. We are inclined to seek out the character of Jewhatred at the phenomenological and historical levels regarding both its origins and its historical recurrences. In a word, our approach to the subject of Jewhatred is historicist. Bauer's proposition, however, makes the opposite claim that Jewhatred is not a matter of time or place at all. Indeed one might even wish to say that the fact of Jewhatred is itself sufficient to justify dismissing historicist claims altogether.

In failing to take account of the distinction between the philosophic and the historical in the study of Jewhatred we also fail to give due consideration to the fundamental and obvious distinction between Jews and Judaism. Most important, the historical and phenomenological approach fails to confront the possibility that the transhistorical character of Jewhatred is somehow related to the transhistorical character of Judaism. But this suggests the quite troubling idea that there is really something to hate or oppose in Judaism. What might the transhistorical element be? Undoubtedly this element is idolatry, that evil, according to Maimonides, against which nearly all the commandments of the Torah are directed.

Insofar as one may say that Judaism stands for the prohibition against idol worship may we not also infer that the substance of Jewhatred may be the worship of idols, or, put another and opposite way, that Jewhatred is a despising of what Judaism calls the One or God? Of course, this can only mean, if true, that the Jewish problem is insoluble as well as infinite in the sense that idolatry, as it is understood in the Second Commandment, is coeval with man's existence. It was in view of considerations of this type that Leo Strauss said: "From every point of view it looks as if the Jewish people were the chosen people, at least in the sense that the Jewish problem is the most manifest symbol of the human problem insofar as it is a social or political problem."[2]

Having posed the question of Jewhatred as a philosophic one it is easy to see why academic scholarship has been unwilling to take it seriously, that is, philosophically. Academic scholarship is not philosophic today but historicist. It is therefore unprepared to consider the possibility that the hatred of Judaism may be a form of idol worship. To consider this possibility would entail a serious consideration of Judaism and of religion simply. This in turn would make it essential to consider the theoretical foundations of modern social science which hold that religious questions are not intrinsically more significant than other questions. In other words, a study of the Jewish Question in history, from the standpoint of idolatry, would expose the suppositions of scholarship to a kind of inquiry that these suppositions were expressly designed to prevent. Moreover, if idolatry is a serious subject for study because the study of religious questions is a serious subject, then there is at least a possibility that suppositions whose purpose it is to foreclose such studies are themselves implicated in religious questions or, *pari passu*, in idolatry.

It will be evident from these observations that the study of Jewhatred from the point of view of idolatry extends beyond the bounds of Judaism as well as beyond the bounds of any single volume or author. The purpose of this book is to indicate the ground of idolatry as lying in the realm of modern ideas of freedom. Freedom is the modern ideal *par excellence*. It has replaced what classical civilization called virtue. In American history where the ideal of freedom has in our time come to possess the character of a dogma in language and in institutional life, the figure of Ralph Waldo Emerson occupies a central position. It was he who made independence or self-reliance – what today is called liberation in popular discourse – his ultimate teaching. By independence or freedom Emerson understood, first of all, that most radical freedom which encompasses both non-dependence (equality) as well as liberty or autonomy. This is the ideal of freedom which, though it is impossible to achieve in the realm of civil existence, has been held out to men in the 20th century as precisely the aim of civil life. The source of this ideal is the founding doctrine of modern thought, the state of nature, according to which each man is his own judge.

Practically speaking the goal of independence has the effect of encouraging centralization in the state as the means to individual liberation. This process involves the destruction of all other or mediating institutions between the individual and the central power.

But this project, reaching to the heart of human institutions, to the self, is ultimately an attack upon reality, and in particular, upon what Emerson called the "terrific Jewish Idea."[3]

Emerson understood better than any previous American and most later ones that the obstacle to freedom was no other than Judaism. In this particular matter we have not paid adequate attention to the reason for Nietzsche's extreme praise of Emerson or to the import of Emerson's most famous and seemingly benign writings on freedom. Our procedure in these pages will be to consider idolatry in its modern setting and to follow a discussion of modern idolatry as such with an analysis of Emerson. Finally we shall consider the ideal of freedom as it has now come to be understood by historical scholars, particularly by David Brion Davis who is among the leading writers to make use of the ideal of modern freedom as both a principle and as the chief subject of American studies. Accordingly we shall begin our study with a consideration of idolatry in its most overt form, namely the Holocaust, whose purpose was, as Hitler said, the absolute annihilation of everything Jewish in existence.[4] Here we take into account the judgment of Emil Fackenheim that Nazism is exactly "false freedom," and represented the "most horrendous idolatry of modern, perhaps of all time."[5] Fackenheim, who is the most profound student of Nazism on the philosophic plane, is especially qualified to discuss idolatry because he has shown himself impervious to the allure of a certain trivialization of the Holocaust which tends to regard the real victim of Jewhatred as "mankind". The cause of Hitler's hatred of Jews was, in this view, not Judaism at all, but a thing much less specific, indeed something that does not exist. Fackenheim has properly disposed of this approach as "an Enlightenment prejudice," in particular it is the prejudice that divides the human vision between a so-called particularist and tribalist principle and a universalist one.

Fackenheim is not persuaded that the real Jew or authentic Judaism is found in what the Stalinist writer Isaac Deutscher called the non-Jewish Jew, that is, in the universalist Jew or in the anti-Jewish, non-ceremonial Jew first attacked by Christians and by the Jew Spinoza. According to the categories of universalism Hitler and Nazism are perceived as reactionary, the enemies of progress, secularism, and democracy. Hitler was among those "demonic enemies," as two Jewish writers who typify this view said recently, of modernity.[6] As for *Mein Kampf*, it is considered "deeply barbarous," a book "to end books."[7] The Third Reich demonstrated once and for all the evil of nationalism or particularism, or hierarchy and authority. Finally, this view asserts that Nazism vindicated an opposite set of principles: egalitarianism, internationalism, and tolerance.

Scholars in fields other than German history, especially if they are Jewish, are prodigal in their use of the Holocaust. A famous example, to which we shall refer at a later time, is Stanley Elkins' astonishing comparison of deathcamp inmates to American slaves. Interestingly, the comparison was offensive to some historians on the ground that slaves did not behave as the Jews were alleged to have done by Elkins. In other words, the comparison of murder and enslavement was not faulted, only the suggestion that slaves behaved like deathcamp inmates. Uses of this type explain in part the popularity of so-called Holocaust studies, a new academic subfield.

In light of this nearly uniform adherence to universalist categories among modern scholars, Fackenheim's study is notable for its daring. He dismisses certain sanctified clichés of Holocaust literature and ignores the taboos of normal political theory. For example, Fackenheim does not suppose that religion is an end equal to all others, but, on the contrary, he agrees with Allan Bloom that it is "the most serious question facing a serious man."[8] In this, Fackenheim offends behaviorists and secular humanists at once. But having done so, Fackenheim is free to disregard as unhistorical and reductionist those accounts of the Holocaust which limit our apprehension of Hitler or of *Mein Kampf* either to the influences upon them or to behavioral inferences from them. Similarly, he does not engage in a certain type of theologizing which, by proposing that the Holocaust demonstrates the non-existence and irrelevance of God, suggests rather the non-existence and irrelevance of any serious Jewish theology.

Fackenheim takes Nazism at its word and considers its deeds in

light of its word. In this he adopts the commonsense approach of
Werner Maser, the outstanding historian of *Mein Kampf*. "To
explain Hitler and to understand the period of history over which he
exerted so decisive an influence," Maser has written, "nothing can
be so important or informative as *Mein Kampf*....Hitler clung
faithfully to the ghastly doctrine set out in *Mein Kampf*."[9]

But the ghastly aspects of *Mein Kampf* are not always the obvious
ones. Hitler was an idealist, or one who is devoted to what modern
liberal scholarship considers the highest goal, freedom. Fackenheim
takes note of Hitler's idealism. The idealistic element in *Mein Kampf*
is not outwardly ghastly. For example, Hitler writes of his wish to
replace one "spiritual" doctrine with another. He does not idolize
force in this matter. "Every attempt at fighting a view of life by
means of force will finally fail," he observed, "unless the fight
against it represents the form of an attack for the sake of a new
spiritual direction." This new spiritual direction is what necessitates
the "thorough eradication" of Jews. Hitler seeks a "new...view of
life."[10]

Hitler's ghastly doctrine aside, he was a moralist. Conversions and
mere persecutions of Jews he regarded as destructive of idealism and
immoral in other respects. Of persecutions he said that, "every
[one]...that takes place without being based on a spiritual
presupposition does not seem justified form the moral point of
view." Traditional Judeophobia failed to express "the character of
an inner and higher consecration, and thus it appeared to many, and
not the worst, as immoral and objectionable. The conviction was
lacking that this was a question of vital importance to the whole of
mankind and that on its solution the fate of all non-Jewish people
depended."[11] Observe how seriously Hitler took the principle of
chosenness.

The eradication of Jews and of all Jewish things Fackenheim
rightly considers to derive from a worshipping of false gods or
idolatry. Nazism sought to make the trinity of Volk, Reich, and
Fuehrer into one. Hitler's purpose was to replace the people who are
representative of the principle that God is One with "eternal
Germanity" as one. In order to establish the significance of idolatry

Fackenheim has recourse to Jewish sources. It is at this point that we confront our wider subject. Idolatry is "false 'freedom,'" in particular, idolatry is the "literal and hence total identification of finiteness with infinitude."[12] What relation exists between ancient idolatry and modern idolators? The ancients were preoccupied with the problems of false worship and false gods. Moderns are secular and do not believe in gods. Fackenheim does not forfeit his fundamental discovery that Nazism is idolatrous by suggesting the Nazis were antimodern pagans. He does not dilute or caricature the rabbinic teaching on idolatry. He insists, on the contrary, that Nazism is "horrendous idolatry."[13] In making this his starting point, Fackenheim assures us that he intends to show that Nazism and its objectives were not trivial. Of course idolatry is not trivial in Jewish terms. It is as we have already said on the authority of Maimonides a counter to Judaism itself. But idolatry is also not trivial in absolute terms. Rather it reflects a disordering of the relationship of man to nature and to the "divine Infinity."

Fackenheim also points out that the ancient rabbis regarded "one who repudiates idolatry...as though he were faithful to the whole Torah. By this standard," says Fackenheim, "any modern Jew would be wholly faithful."[14] But it goes without saying that modern Jews are not wholly faithful even though they do repudiate the worship of idols or images. Does this not indicate the irrelevance of the rabbinic teaching, and by implication the irrelevance of Judaism? Fackenheim refers to the following talmudic passage, a characteristic utterance regarding idolatry, to suggest why such questions are not well-founded.

> When someone in his anger tears his clothes, breaks utensils, throws away money, this should be viewed as though he worshipped idols. For this is the cunning of the evil inclination: today it says 'do this,' tomorrow, 'do that,' until it finally says 'go and worship idols' and he goes and does it....What is the alien god that dwells in a man's body? The evil inclination.[15]

The danger of idol worship is not the "ludicrous anticlimax" moderns suppose.[16] Instead those who believe they are not subject to idol worship because they are indifferent to the gods have fallen prey to idolatry without even knowing it was a temptation. In the case of Nazism, Fackenheim explains, idol worship is based in the same feelings as ancient idol worship, that is, in "infinite fear, hope, pleasure or pain."[17] But the object of worship in Nazism, namely the unity of Hitler, Volk, and Reich, is not recognized as an idol. On the contrary this object is understood to bring about the liberation from "idolatrous thralldom."[18] In other words, modern idolatry understands itself to be liberation or "demythologization." As Fackenheim puts it, "the truth in this new false 'freedom' is that, negating all worship, it negates all idolatry in the form of worship. This new idolator takes himself for an enlightened modern."[19] Moreover, because the modern idolator is enlightened, he scorns idols as mere sticks and stones at the same time that he condemns all worship as superfluous. But the idolatrous essence, the identification of finiteness and infinitude, survives like the duck inside the wolf in the tale of Peter. "Because [the infinite feeling of the modern idolator] is infinite, it does not vanish....It thus acquires the power of generating what may be called *internalized idolatry*."[20]

Fackenheim recognizes two forms of modern "internalized" idolatry and distinguishes "internalized religion" from both. Hitler's idolatry Fackenheim calls "idealistic." It identifies finiteness with infinitude in making the finite infinite. Nazism is "absolute whim...the extreme in finitude."[21] Naturalistic or empiricist idolatry is marked by positivist and relativistic "anti-absolutism." It identifies finiteness with infinitude in making the infinite finite; the "degradation of the infinite aspect of selfhood to a false finitude." The so-called value-free perverters of Dewey and Freud, but not Dewey or Freud themselves, are naturalist idolators according to Fackenheim because they deny all goals, including even those of Dewey and Freud that "man should make himself into the natural being he is."[22]

Internalized religion is carefully distinguished from idolatry, whether of the idealistic or naturalistic sort. It would be "a fatal error to confuse" internalized religion and internalized idolatry, says Fackenheim.[23] The knowing denial of the divine Infinity, that is, the "raising [of an individual or a collective self] to infinity in...[the] very act of denial," is "internalized religion," not "internalized idolatry," when this denial "issues, not in an atheistic rejection of the Divine, but rather in its internalization."[24] This situation, although it "raises the specter of a modern, internalized idolatry," is kept from becoming idolatry in the "modern...philosophies...[of] Fichte, Schelling, Hegel," because "finiteness and infinitude are...kept firmly apart." And, what is true of these "idealist" philosophers is also true of the "humanistic atheists...Feuerbach, Marx and Nietzsche." The identification of finiteness and infinitude is here "as firmly (if not as obviously) rejected...by the fact that Divinity vanishes in the process of internalization, to be replaced by a humanity potentially infinite in its modern 'freedom'....The potentiality never seems to become quite actual." In sum, internalized religion is an "authentic challenge" to the divine Infinity which should be respected by Jewish and Christian thinkers. Internalized idolatry, on the other hand, is "demonic perversion."[25] Above all, this distinction is rooted in the "honest rationality" of the philosophers. Unlike idolatrous parodies of thought which are "the product, not of reason, but of passion," the philosophers are not idolatrous.[26] Nazism, internalized idolatry, is a denial of the divine Infinity. At the same time it is a literal and hence total identification of finiteness with infinitude. Although Hitler was "no emperor-god...and the Volk, no worshipping community," yet the "will of a Fuehrer" and the will of the Volk were the sole reality. The object of idol worship is the will, internalized in Volk and Fuehrer who are one. Nazism is a "bastard-child of...the Enlightenment."[27]

Fackenheim has undoubtedly pointed us in the direction of uncovering the source of the Holocaust's mystery, therefore of the mystery of Jewhatred. The ground of idolatry or the identification of finitude and infinity is false freedom. But Fackenheim's further distinction between internalized idolatry and internalized religion is not sound. We shall miss entirely the deeply paradoxical hints Emerson gives us about self-reliance, as well as such denunciations of Judaism by so representative a modern writer as David Brion Davis, if we exempt "internalized religion" from Fackenheim's valuable conception.

The philosopher's impulse, which does not deny the divine Infinity but which seeks only to bring the divine, "as it were...in[to] the same inner space as the human self," is surely an idolatrous aspiration.[28] More important, this impulse participates in the same aspiration which informs such demonic perversions as Nazism.

Fackenheim's distinction between internalized religion and internalized idolatry is outwardly commonsensical in that thought is always different from action. But this difference is especially inappropriate as a distinction in the case of the great philosophies, all of which sought to identify thought and act at some level. Commonsensical as well is the unmistakable difference between any of the great philosophies and the comparatively low level theorizing of Hitler. But differences of this type have no philosophical relevance. Moreover, Fackenheim is himself compelled to recognize the, to him, quite troubling compatibility of Heidegger and Nazism.

Heidegger's was "one of the profoundest philosophies of this century," Fackenheim observes, and surely he was an exponent of internalized religion. As late as 1946, however, Heidegger failed to recognize "radical evil" in the Holocaust. Fackenheim considers this failure a "philosophical" one, not a challenge to the distinction between internalized religion and internalized idolatry.[29] But Fackenheim does not explain how Heidegger's "philosophical failure" differs from idolatry. One wonders if perhaps there is no distinction between this philosophical failure and idolatry or, put another way, if there really is a distinction between internalized idolatry and internalized religion. Let it be noted here, before we consider this possibility, that historically at least there is no reason to suppose any such distinction ever existed. Karl Löwith has observed that "nihilism as the disavowal of existing civilization," and not internalized religion, "was the only belief of all truly educated people at the beginning of the twentieth century."[30]

We need not be concerned here with the subject of nihilism except to note the indisputable fact that Hitler explicitly disavowed existing civilization and identified it with Judaism. Certainly it is this disavowal that Heidegger found "great" in Nazism. As for Heidegger's own disavowals of antisemitism, they cannot be given much weight as evidence of a philosophic intention as against an idolatrous one. The tradition of modern philosophy is, of course, marked by hostility to Judaism, as Fackenheim's study, among others, shows, even as this hostility is almost always hedged about with the liberal's disdain for all "prejudice," especially for antisemitism.

A final observation about the great philosophies considered from the standpoint of Fackenheim's defense of the distinction between internalized idolatry and internalized religion is the supposed "authenticity" of the great philosophies. Consider that Fackenheim exempts Hegel from an idolatrous identification of finitude and infinity, saying he "reaches the Fichtean goal [of a divinized moral self], but does so in the realm of thought only."[31] Marx too is no idolator, according to Fackenheim. Insofar as the theorist of world communism realized that "society [is] as yet far from classless," he did not identify the finite and the infinite.[32] But one may question if these are plausible distinctions or authentic ones. Can Hegel or Marx, of all thinkers, be defended on the ground that the idolatrous tendency of an identification of finitude and infinity was not idolatrous because it was limited to the realm of thought? Precisely the identification of thought and act was their objective. Hegel did not doubt the realm of thought would succeed to action, in particular to the universal state. Certainly Marx did not scorn the prospect of a classless society. The distinction Fackenheim insists upon is here again not a theoretical but a circumstantial and historical one. One must look rather far to find a more pertinent example of internalized idolatry, a knowing identification of the divine Infinity dwelling in a man, than Hegel's *Wissenschaft der Logik*:

> [The] Logic is to be understood as the system of pure reason, as the realm of pure thought. This realm is the truth as it is without veil and [for itself]. It can be said, therefore, that this is the exposition of God as he is in his eternal essence, before the creation of nature and a finite mind.[33]

We may not say of Hegel that he has taken "care [that]...the possibility of idolatry is...recognized and avoided."[34] It is the judgment of Alexandre Kojève, Hegel's best known 20th century leftwing expositor, and we believe his most acute expositor of any persuasion, that Hegel was nothing less than God, a claim we shall look into in due course.[35]

But the distinction Fackenheim would have us credit between the great philosophies and demonic perversions of them rests on what is itself a fatal error. Honest rationality, said to separate products of reason from those of passion, in fact confounds reason and passion.

Concerning the distinction between reason and passion, it must at least be noted that the tide of modern political philosophy, in which Leo Strauss noted three waves, is dominated by philosophies of passion.[36] Beginning with Machiavelli, who substituted glory for virtue, and Hobbes, who replaced glory with power, the great philosophies have been notable for their rejections of reason, whether in hallowing folk minds as expressions of a general will or in the sanctification of history as an expression of nature or idea. In the third and present wave of modernity inaugurated by Nietzsche, the West has been inclined to think "that all human life and human thought ultimately rests on horizon-forming creations which are not susceptible of rational legitimization."[37]

This historical consideration regarding passion and reason is not irrelevant to the distinction Fackenheim asks us to accept between the philosophies and Hitler. We live at a time when it is the nearly universal presumption of political thinkers that man is not a political being but is instead an amorphous or "free" being, to be shaped by history, by labor or by change. This presumption, a reversal of the understanding of Aristotle that man is a political being, is related to another Aristotelian principle which modern political thinkers have also reversed. This principle is that "the mind is moved by the mover."[38] Reason, in other words, the ancients regarded as "revelation," not as a thing man-made. These two related reversals of classical thought by moderns bear directly on our subject. They are the bases for modern idolatry and for the too easy supposition that idolatry is not a modern possibility, or that honest rationality is a hedge against it. The identification of finitude and infinity in Nietzsche, one of Fackenheim's great philosophers, is complete because the identification of making and thinking is complete.

In Nietzsche, thought is action, in particular it is vitalism. When Nietzsche internalizes the divine infinity (or the One), his idolatry is not simply in the realm of thought. It is palpable idolatry because thought is act in Nietzsche: "The greatest events – they are not our loudest but our stillest hours. Not around the inventors of new noise, but around the inventors of new values does the world revolve; it revolves *inaudibly*."[39] And Zarathustra counsels: " 'Will to truth'....A will to the thinkability of all beings; this *I* call your will. You want to *make* all being thinkable."[40] Nietzsche's method qualifies as rational insofar as it is autonomous and free, but its essence is passion. What is art in Nietzsche is system in Max Weber. Weber is the formulator of the principle of honest rationality as the basis for the distinction between morality or idealism and immorality, the distinction informing Fackenheim's defense of the great philosophies.

Weber's distinction between idealism and immorality derives in part, as will be clear shortly, from his conviction that facts and values are heterogeneous. It is not irrelevant to add that Weber's teaching that only facts are knowable while all judgments regarding values are relative continues to inform both a naturalistic social science in which "value judgments" are impermissible, and a neo-Kantian and secular humanism in which the facts are said to be value-laden. Academic social studies, in other words, must also be affected by the critique of honest rationality.

The context of Fackenheim's invocation of honest rationality is Weberian. But in a critique of Weber of the profoundest kind, Strauss has shown the falsity of the distinction between products of reason and of passion fashioned by honest rationality.[41] Honest rationality, or the principle of freedom according to which one is free in the degree that he is "guided by rational consideration of means and ends," is said to be nihilistic.[42] Strauss's critique of Weber bears directly and with great force upon the question of idolatry.

According to Weber, reason, particularly in the determining of moral imperatives which appeal to intellect (unlike merely cultural or personal values and wants to which our feelings are subject), is the glory and dignity of man. Not choosing and not valuing is the equivalent of appetitiveness and passion. "Man's dignity, his being exalted far above all brutes, consists in his setting up autonomously his ultimate values, in making these values his constant ends, and in rationally choosing the means to these ends. The dignity of man consists in his...freely choosing his own values or his own ideals."[43] Commitment to a value which appeals to our reason Weber counted idealism.

But Strauss reminds us that the justification for this view of idealism is a scientific understanding of values, that is, an understanding that facts are possessed of transhistorical or universal character while values are relative and discrete. Because the truth about values is said to be inaccessible, a scientific and rational as well as an honest approach to values must be neutrality toward values. And yet indifference to all values is what Weber counts as baseness. Freedom and rationality suggest a rational hostility toward theory. But this would mean an espousal of unfreedom or passion. It is no accident that this hostility to values and to theory is embodied in naturalistic social science (behaviorism), and in the value-laden humanism which frequently opposes it, that is, in those two forms of academic social studies that grew out of Weber's distinction between facts and values. Thus, the positivist regards theory as unempirical. He makes indifference to all causes or "openness" a cause. At the opposite extreme stands the humanist who dignifies all causes in the name of freedom and dignity regardless of whether a cause appeals to our mind or to our passion. "A cause that appeals no further than 'the sphere of one's own individuality,'" the vitalism of Nietzsche, counts as a cause.[44] The first position is formalistic and self-canceling, and the second is simply a doctrine of power. Weber, in sum, having undertaken the defense of idealism as freedom and commitment to a value, ultimately dignifies mere personal preferences and willing as idealistic. Idealism is here the merest formalism: any cause counts as idealistic. Our culture has institutionalized this version of idealism as it appears at the level of popular expression in any number of relativistic formulas. We tend to credit any idealism, however base or fanatical, if only the idealist is sincere and committed to his views.

The distinction between idealism and appetitiveness fades into freedom as such, as the distinction between values and facts, ought and is, collapses into an identity of ought and is. The final formulation of Weber's ethical principle would then be " 'Thou shalt have preferences' – an Ought whose fulfillment is fully guaranteed by the Is."[45] Honest rationality, the choosing of values as called for by intellect as against acceptance of values which appeal to our feelings, is obviously arbitrary. Why be honest or rational? Reason and passion, idealism and appetitiveness are morally equal on the principle of honest rationality, or rather there is no such principle.

Fackenheim's distinction between the great philosophies and Hitler is subject to the same nihilistic consequence attaching to the distinction between idealism and immorality in Weber. This would suggest that the distinction between internalized religion and internalized idolatry is also inadequate. In fact, Fackenheim has not done full justice to the rabbinic teaching, perhaps because he has done more than full justice to the great philosophies.

Fackenheim's critique of the rabbinic teaching does not do full justice to Judaism. Certainly the rabbis would not have supposed that the false freedom of the great philosophers in bringing the divine Infinity into the same space with a human being was an "authentic challenge" to be taken seriously as religious and not idolatrous. The rabbis were not liberals for whom challenges to the divine Infinity counted as authentic. One cannot maintain that Nazism is idolatrous while consenting to an Hellenic gloss on the rabbinic teaching. That "the Hellenic spirit of free inquiry...is not rooted in Judaism," as Husik has correctly observed, is a fact moderns find difficult to accept.[46] Concerning the subject of idolatry, one might even say that this spirit of what moderns call free inquiry is the essence of the *yetzer hara*, the evil inclination. The divine Infinity which occupies the same inner space with the philosopher cannot be God. Such an occupant, the rabbis say, is precisely "the alien god." This is the god that says, "do anything," i.e., be free. Freedom, or the evil inclination, is the alien god. In a word, freedom, understood as "false freedom," is idolatry, even though we know it is today "a mark of intelligence and progress...[to praise] serious consideration of alien gods."[47] "Internalization" has been the rabbinic interpretation from the start. Is it not for this reason that the Second Commandment, as Cynthia Ozick has said, "runs against the grain of our social nature, indeed against human imagination"?[48] Let us note here as well what Emerson counseled regarding the command that men not "take the name of God in vain." He said: "You cannot say God, blood, & hell too little. Always suppose God. The Jew named him not." (JMN, IX, 273) Emerson's project or freedom envisaged, as in *Nature*, the vanishing of reality and its replacement by "your own world."[49]

Notes

1. Quoted in *The Los Angeles Times*, 9 November 1981.

2. Leo Strauss, *Liberalism Ancient and Modern* (Chicago, 1960), 230.

3. William Gilman, *et al.*, eds., *The Journals and Miscellaneous Notebooks of Ralph Waldo Emerson* (Cambridge, Massachusetts, 1960–), VII, 32; henceforth abbreviated as JMN in the text.

4. Adolf Hitler, *Mein Kampf* (New York, 1925, 1927 [1939]), 221.

5. Emil Fackenheim, *Encounters Between Judaism and Modern Philosophy: Preface to Future Jewish Thought* (New York, 1973), 175.

6. Paul R. Mendes-Flohr and Yehuda Reinharz, eds., *The Jew in the Modern World: A Documentary History* (New York, 1980), vii.

7. Dorothy Thompson, "A Review of *Mein Kampf*" in "Books", *New York Herald Tribune*, 19 March 1939.

8. Allan Bloom, "The Study of Texts," in Melvin Richter, ed., *Political Theory and Political Education* (Princeton, 1980), 122.

9. Werner Maser, *Hitler's "Mein Kampf": an Analysis* (London, 1970), 11.

10. Hitler, *Mein Kampf*, 221.

11. Ibid., 155–156.

12. Fackenheim, *Encounters*, 189.

13. Ibid., 175.

14. Ibid., 173.

15. Quoted in ibid., 178.

16. Ibid., 179.

17. Ibid., 217.

18. Ibid., 187.

19. Ibid.

20. Ibid.

21. Ibid., 194.

22. Ibid., 196.

23. Ibid., 190.

24. Ibid., 191.

25. Ibid., 190.

26. Ibid., 192.

27. Ibid., 197, 187.

28. Ibid., 191, 194.

29. Ibid., 217, 223.

30. Karl Löwith, *Nature, History, and Existentialism* (Evanston, Illinois, 1966), 10.

31. Fackenheim, *Encounters*, 191.

32. Ibid.

33. G.W.F. Hegel, *Science of Logic* (New York, 1969), 50.

34. Fackenheim, *Encounters*, 190.

35. Alexandre Kojève, *Introduction to the Reading of Hegel, Lectures on the Phenomenology of the Spirit* (New York, 1969).

36. Leo Strauss, "What is Political Philosophy?" in *What is Political Philosophy and Other Studies* (Glencoe, Illinois, 1959), 9–55.

37. Ibid., 54.

38. Aristotle, *Metaphysics*, 1072a30.

39. Friedrich Nietzsche, *Thus Spoke Zarathustra* in Walter Kaufmann, ed., *The Portable Nietzsche* (New York, 1954), 243.

40. Ibid., 225.

41. Leo Strauss, *Natural Right and History* (Chicago, 1953), 35–80.

42. Ibid., 44.

43. Ibid.

44. Ibid., 46.

45. Ibid.

46. I.Husik, "Hellenism and Judaism," *Philosophical Essays* (Oxford, 1952), 13.

47. Harry Neumann, "Torah or Philosophy? Jewish Alternatives to Modern Epicureanism," *The Journal of Value Inquiry*, XI (1977), 23.

48. Cynthia Ozick, "Judaism and Harold Bloom," *Commentary*, 67 (1979), 51.

49. Robert E. Spiller, *et al.*, eds., *The Collected Works of Ralph Waldo Emerson* (2 vols.; Cambridge, Massachusetts, 1971, 1979), I, 45; henceforth abbreviated CW in the text. Citations from Edward Waldo Emerson, ed., *The Complete Works of Ralph Waldo Emerson* (12 vols.; Boston 1903–1904) will be abbreviated in text as W. The following parenthetical abbreviations will be used: "American Scholar" ("AS"); "Circles" ("C"); "Compensation" ("CM"); "Divinity School Address" ("DSA"); "History" ("H"); "Intellect" ("I"); "Method of Nature" ("MN"); "Montaigne; or the Skeptic" ("MS"); *Nature* (*N*); "Over–Soul" ("OS"); "Plato" ("P"); "Self-Reliance" ("SR").

CHAPTER 2

Freedom and the Jewish Question

The Jewish teaching on false freedom is not ambiguous. False freedom is false Exodus from Egypt. It is the making of the golden calf while Moses is at Sinai preparing to deliver the Torah, or true freedom, to Israel. Modern idolatry takes two forms. First is the idolatry associated with the consideration of man as an animal lacking reason and a soul. Here man exits from or escapes his condition as a being of more than animal elements. Let us call this form of idolatry the Melian exodus, following Eric Voegelin, who locates the contraction of man's being into a "power-self" as the means of "concupiscential exodus" in the Melian dialogue detailed by Thucydides.[1] There is, in addition to the Melian exodus, a second embodiment of idolatry, or gnostic exodus. In gnosticism, men renounce the trappings of their mortality, including history and culture, in an attempt to bring about, at God's expense, the conditions of perfection symbolized in the garden of Eden. At the level of popular and of academic discourse, these embodiments of idolatry are understood in the language of political jargon as Right and Left. This language does not intend religious meanings. Nonetheless, the present purpose is to suggest that conventional political discourse misunderstands the difference of Right and Left, which it considers only political. The division, and opposition, of Right (Melian) and Left (gnostic) is idolatry in its modern form.

It goes without saying that a judgment that Right and Left touch religious aspects is offensive to much political science. But not all scholars are content that religious questions should be divorced from political theory. Allan Bloom has observed that "what is perhaps the most serious question facing a serious man – the religious question – is almost a matter of indifference" to political writers in our time.[2] This indifference is found in John Rawls, for example, whose study of equality is one of a handful of major works in political science. But Rawls regards religion as "just another one of the many ends that can be pursued in a liberal society."[3]

Again it is Bloom who has pointed out that modern political writing which evades the serious questions also evades the easy historical ones, inviting sloppiness and errors of fact.[4] One may say, however, that what is most consistently mistaken by modern writers such as Rawls is the involvement of political writing in idolatry. Rawls's equation of all ends is precisely idolatry of the gnostic type. Knowledge that all ends or values are equal is not a human possibility, but a divine one. Again it is useful to point out the form this doctrine has assumed in our popular culture, for example in the expression of radical toleration. Here the appearance of an anti-dogmatic and openminded approach disguises what is in reality the opposite. The tolerant speaker claims to know, prior to all factual and ethical considerations, that all moral answers are equal as to their truth, that is, all truth claims are relative. Yet must not metaphysics and religion, dealing with questions about ends, be more serious than other pursuits in a liberal society or in any society? If Nazism is idolatry, a political science such as that of Rawls is precluded from studying it. One cannot undertake a study of Nazism as idolatry in the context of modern political science because this science is implicated in idolatry. The following survey of Nazism as idolatrous suggests the nature of this implication.

The idolatry in Nazism is found in connection with the biblical teaching on freedom. The story of the Exodus is an explication of true and false freedom. True freedom is the recognition of God, and the recognition that follows from the recognition of God. It is that man is radically distinct from animals and from God. Man is neither raw desire nor spirit. He is in between or in the metaxy, to use a pertinent Platonic term that we have use for later on. False freedom, in contrast, is the freedom or exodus from the metaxy, symbolized in the making of the golden calf by which men simultaneously attempt to be gods themselves and to sanctify raw desire.

The Exodus of the Jewish people is plainly not one from Egypt but to Israel. Exodus from Egypt is marked above all by wandering and by a desert. Moreover, the Exodus from Egypt and the opening of the Red Sea are not effected by the Jews but by God. The Exodus is no war of national liberation. Most important, to consider the Exodus as though it were a mere war of liberation from Egyptian bondage is idolatry. Thus, when the Israelites make the golden calf they proclaim: "These are your Gods, O Israel, which brought you up out of the land of Egypt."[5] But this is false; the golden calf was newly made by the Jews. But then who split the Red Sea if not God or the golden calf? Naturally, it must have been the Jews: God is a projection or superstition; freedom is man's work and man is the maker. Exodus is then freedom or the exercise of human will: absolute whim. It is the liberation to do as one lists, to wander. Exodus is the freedom not to wait for Moses: to go to Israel or not. But of course the Bible teaches that this is all false.

The calf makers are idol worshippers and are slain. They have forfeited reason by equating their whim or freedom with rationality. They made the same error that Strauss detected in Weberian idealism or honest rationality. And, as in the Weberian instance, the mistaking of whim for rationality is equivalent to animality or mere desiring. The calf makers are considered as animals. In one of the most famous expositions of idolatry in the Bible, Nebuchadnezzar is punished with the loss of his reason and sent to forage in the manner of oxen for his failure, demonstrated in his making of a golden idol, to recognize that "the most High rules in the Kingdom of man."[6] But Nebuchadnezzar, this great enemy of the Jews, appears in Emerson as a hero. Moreover, Emerson's conception of reason is that men must liberate themselves from reality.

But reason understood to be that which finds its source in the revelation that God and not man is the maker of all things, can distinguish between exodus as false and as true freedom. A calf is a thing. All things perish. Things come into being and go out of being. The bush that burns but is not consumed is a sign of divinity because it does not perish. Being remains, namely, the process of coming into being and going out of being remains. This process is known only to man who alone among things possesses reason or soul. This permits him to see the sign of the burning bush and to understand it. This recognition indicates that aspect of man's being, spirit or soul, which is not a thing. We call this aspect of perception immortality.

Freedom is false when men pretend they are animals or gods. The literal and hence total identification of finiteness and infinitude is a form of idolatry because such identification is a willful disordering of reality. Idolatry is the knowing denial of the doctrine which founds Judaism, or monotheism: "Hear, O Israel, the Lord is your God, the Lord is One."[7] The biblical exposition of this principle, set in the Exodus or Passover story, specifies idolatry as false freedom or exodus from the metaxy. There are two modes of exodus or false freedom.

Men may escape the metaxy or the conditions of human being in the direction Fackenheim calls naturalism by identifying as finite those aspects of being that are infinite. The insistence that man is an animal who invents God for the sake of satisfying behavioral imperatives is idolatrous in this sense. The value-free principle is a doctrine of raw power, as are its derivatives, for example, the "open society," and certain versions of equality and free speech. Justice, which regards all value claims as equal, is achievable only by enforcement of absolute toleration and permissiveness or by enforcement of sameness and intolerance in the name of humanity. Force is inevitable in either case to insure absolute permissiveness or absolute conformity, since it cannot be the case that values will not clash, or that self-control will be considered a value superior to others.

In fact, the sole means of avoiding the arbitrary dilemma of tolerance is to undertake a transformation of the self, that is, to undertake the elimination of the self or amour propre. In other words, this doctrine of freedom entails a reordering of the relationship of the One and the many whether in the reformation of selves into a general will or into Ein Volk, Ein Reich, Ein Fuehrer. As we shall see in Hitler's case, work makes free because it destroys egotism. In particular, freedom as work eliminates rewards based upon skill. The individual is thus merged into the collective self. Freedom from values as the meaning of freedom is simply power or will. We have already called this freedom from values the Melian exodus, after Thucydides: "Men...rule wherever they can."[8]

Hitler's conception of right was certainly Melian. Alan Bullock, who has called this aspect of Hitler's thought "crude Darwinism," notes that "no word occurs more frequently in Hitler's speeches than 'struggle.'" "The whole work of Nature," according to Hitler, is "a mighty struggle." Again: "The first fundamental of any rational Weltanschauung is the fact that on earth and in the universe, force alone is decisive."[9]

Voegelin explains that the "fictitious identity of conquest with reality can be achieved by identifying reality with a humanity contracted to its libidinous self."[10] The modern forms of this aspect of false freedom, according to which so-called values, and thus judgments concerning them, are historical and ultimately identical to personal desire, are embodied in historicisms of mind or spirit. In other words, Melian exodus denies to philosophy all but historical and pragmatic aptitudes. The difference between the ancient and modern expressions of this exodus is the hint of tragic fatality in the ancient forms and the absence of this hint in modern ones. The Athenian conquerors retain, "in the background...the tragic consciousness of the process." They too will be massacred in time. Modern movements, on the other hand, sink "to the untragic vileness of the ideologist who cannot commit the murder he wants to commit in order to gain an 'identity' in place of the self he has lost, without moralistically appealing to a dogma of ultimate truth."[11]

The dogma to which Hitler appealed was the thousand-year Reich, eternal Germany. This vision he conceived as freedom and the elimination of Judaism. Freedom and the replacement of Judaism with Germany would prepare the way for a reconciliation of mankind. These objectives were exactly dogmas of ultimate truth for the sake of committing murders. Moreover, these dogmas were the instruments for the formation of selves.

We need not doubt Hilter used the word "struggle" many times or that he identified morality with power. But his object was not solely power. His murderous intention was not arbitrary or irrational. Hitler's doctrine of the blood is the key to the other side of Nazism and simultaneously to the idolatrous aspect of the great philosophies.

Hitler's notorious sacrifice of military goals so as to destroy the million Jews of Hungary reflects his commitment to the doctrine of the blood. The doctrine of the blood is an inversion of the doctrine of the soul. Speaking often of "our people" and "eternal Germanity," Hitler's purpose was to effect the "reconciliation of mankind," or "all non-Jewish peoples." Nazism emerges as a counter-Judaism at this point. The "purity of the blood...[will] enable our people to mature for the fulfillment of the mission which the Creator of the universe has allotted also to them." This, the "higher motive of national policy and never narrow particularism" explains why the "State has nothing whatsoever to do with a definite conception of economics or development of economics."[12] Nazism was a moral doctrine of freedom for which race was the form.

As persecution of the Jews was immoral in Hitler's thinking, so the purity of German blood was not a medical or an anthropological doctrine, even though it had import at such levels. One suspects we hear neither the hypocrite nor the psychopath say, as Hitler did in 1932, "Let them call us unhuman. If we save Germany, we shall have done the greatest deed in the world....Let them say that we are without morality. If our people is saved, we shall have paved the way for morality."[13] The doctrine of the blood introduces the gnostic aspect of Nazism.

Hitler's identification of right with power included the second mode of exodus from the metaxy, or gnosticism. But the liberation of the spirit from the body in modern gnosticism is not for rare men or for the elite as among ancient gnostics. The modern way of liberation is release from the ego and egotism. The spirit, in other words, is not private vision, it is a shared thing, for example, blood.

Modern gnosticism is distinguished from its ancient forms in the same way that modern power politics differs from Melian exodus of the ancients. For the ancient gnostic who strove to separate the soul from things, the instrument of liberation was the individual. The soul with its source in the divine was not thus denied even though this immanentization or the bringing of God into a human space permitted men to suppose they were gods. Liberation of the souls of modern gnostics is altogether a thing of groups that replace the divine as the soul's source. Accordingly modern gnosticism calls for the losing of the self as spirit. The soul of modern man is liberated from the prison of spirit, as well as the prison of the body, in becoming a thing that does not perish, i.e., in submerging the ego in an immortalizing thing such as blood, sex, or excrement.

Consider Hitler's doctrine in connection with the tradition regarding the self extending from Rousseau. Since Rousseau's description of the self as formed by society, in particular by the division of labor and the advent of property, there has evolved the idea that one's authentic self lies beneath the roles imposed by social life. Liberation is then a release from property and its social and other derivatives. This conception takes its rise in the doctrine of the state of nature holding that man has no nature or telos. True personality or selfhood is freedom as such, or becoming. This vision of freedom also imposes a conception of the self as selfless. Selflessness or true selfhood is tantamount to compassion, and this is how Rousseau defined it. The good self is not selfish in a literal and a moral sense. The true self is not an I, but we. This reversal of the classical and Jewish concept of the self is part of everyday speech in which a self is virtuous if it is selfless.

It is by no means irrelevant to point out here that this vision is explicit in American history. In Emerson's time especially and in the abolitionist movement we find much explicit celebration of selflessness. An important example in the antebellum period is John Humphrey Noyes who "hoped to extinguish the pronoun I" to be replaced by "the we spirit."[14] More recently writers such as Norman O. Brown have proclaimed that the "boundary line between self and the external world bears no relation to reality." Liberation for Brown is release from self by means of return to the pre-socialized conditions of polymorphous perversity. The "human consciousness can be liberated from the parental (Oedipal) complex only by being liberated from its cultural derivatives, the paternalistic state and the patriarchal God."[15]

This conception of self, including the role of man as maker of God, is the one we have detected in Nazism. The liberation from God, thus the liberation of the self, establishes the idea of freedom, of exodus from the metaxy. The power to free the soul from the body is brought about by freeing the self from an I. The I perishes. What remains is a thing possessed of the characteristics of God, that is, of oneness. Those basic and selfless elements which outlast the individual have become the instruments of immortality. What perishes excessively – excrement, sexuality, blood – are now the bases for oneness and everlasting life. Donatien de Sade uncovered these principles two centuries before Hitler put them into practice. "What we call the end of the living," said Sade (in praise of the motto that "the freest of people are they who are most friendly to murder"), "is no longer a true finis, but a simple transformation...of matter....[D]eath is hence no more than a change of form, an imperceptible passage from one existence into another."[16] Here in palpable form is the identification of finitude with the infinite exposed by Fackenheim. But Hitler is not a "parody" of the great philosophers. In assuming a material and communal replacement of the divine as the source of man's freedom, Hitler's attack upon Judaism substitutes German blood for the soul. Hitler would in this way immortalize or make infinite a finite thing. Hitler insists that Judaism is the negation of German blood – Judaism is a race, not a religion – exactly as Marx insists that Judaism is the negation of communism – the god of Judaism, he says, is money. But if we consider, in Hitler's case, the actual doctrine of blood in Judaism where it serves as a symbol of the soul, Hitler's gnostic intention stands out boldly.

The Nazi's blood was his soul. As a Jewish symbol that had become an object of worship, the Nazi doctrine of the blood is in truth "an absolute falsehood."[17] The blood as a substitute for the soul of man is false. In Judaism the blood is typically considered to be in the soul only when the body is alive. "The flesh whose blood is still in its soul, shall ye not eat....Blood...belongs to your souls."[18] This is plainly because the soul is not a thing. Preservation of the blood of generations, what Hitler believed to be the Jews' purpose, and what he hoped to make the German purpose, was to create oneness and immortality, as it were, the salvation of souls. Jewish pollution of the racial stock of others, imperiling the survival of non-Jewish humanity, robbed souls by interruption of the transmission of blood. In Nazism the soul is in the blood. The soul is preserved after the ego dies, and because it is, the race is preserved.

The doctrine of blood is false because it is wholly a distortion of the order of being. The source of human freedom is not the absence of the divine and its replacement by a Nazi or a communist community. It is hardly a coincidence that both Hitler and Marx considered the elimination of Jews and Judaism to be a condition for the establishment of their projects.[19] In both cases the extinguishment of the divine in the name of a man-made creation of freedom and of human being is critical. The racist aspect of Nazism and the scientific and class aspects of communism are perhaps best described as opiates for the proletariat and the intelligentsia respectively.

The blood is then the soul made matter, an absurd idea. The characteristic of the soul is immortality. What can it mean to proclaim that the soul is not spiritual or that some thing, perishable by definition, is immortal? What aspect of a person does not perish? The answer, embodied in the doctrine of the blood is: that aspect of a person which is neither an ego nor a soul. Of course there is no such thing. But what did Hitler think this thing was? Of course he supposed it was freedom. The masses shall enter into the service of freedom once they understand that the Jew intends the "enslavement and with it the destruction, of all non-Jewish peoples."[20] Blood is the oneness of soul of the German people. Oneness will come about by the destruction of vanity or egotism, the opposite of oneness.

Egotism must be destroyed. But how is this possible? By destroying the people of egotism. This is the people that hides behind a false, unenlightened doctrine of election and the divine as One.

This people, the representative of the false God of spirit, and therefore the enemy of oneness or the German people, is the Jews. "The Jew is the mortal enemy of our people," said Hitler, because "the Jew is...nothing but pure egoism."[21] And thus this destruction of Jews is part of the means for liberation, namely work. The people become one as they give their egos over to the community. The doctrine that man is one is egalitarianism.

"Egalitarianism," said Erich Fromm, writing in defense of Marx's attack upon Judaism as the obstacle to the community of mankind, "is not sameness but oneness."[22] Hitler's doctrine is egalitarian in the deepest and purest modern sense. As such, Nazism is the most complete distillation of modernity. When Hitler proclaims that "the Jew forms the strongest contrast to the Aryan" because only the Aryan is willing to give his "life for the existence of the community," he intends to be taken at his word.[23] Giving up one's life for the community calls for the relinquishment of ego. The means for doing so is of course not prayer. Everyone knows, Hitler said, "a nation cannot be freed by prayer."[24] Rather the way to freedom is work. Work creates oneness in the process of effacing egos. Work "establish[es] the equality of all in the moment when every individual endeavors to do the best in his field....It is on this that the evaluation of man must rest, and not on the reward."[25] Work makes free. Hitler promises freedom from the ego, that is, from death, from anxiety, by promising immortality in this world. This is the meaning of Hitler's doctrine of the blood. It is the foundation of the "everlasting [German] people."[26]

It is correct to say, with Fackenheim, that Hitler is no emperor-god; nor are the Volk a worshipping community. It is Germanity in its immortalizing sacrifice of egos that is God or one. This is the everlasting German people in whose name Hitler professed to speak. The Jews, who are said to live on behalf of an everlasting God, the God who is one because man and all things are many, are the obvious spiritual power to be destroyed.

Hitler's idolatry is unmistakable. It reflects a disordering of the relationship of the One and the many. Man is enjoined, in the name of salvation, to leave his place in the metaxy that he may assume full freedom. In the language of political science Hitler's Melian exodus is fascist or rightwing. Here only power counts because all values are equal, making law the rule of the stronger. Man is an animal. To this, Hitler's obvious or familiar side, is added the other more subtle and as it were saintlier side. This is the idolatry of gnosticism whereby men singly or together take God into themselves or into their ideals.

Hitler's case suggests that modern idolatry cannot fail to be both Melian and gnostic. We do not often, however, credit Hitler's gnosticism or realize the Melian aspects of gnostic or liberal idealism when it is expressed in the seductive language of opposition to Melian realism. The position of Judaism is obviously not the only representative of the principles idolatry must oppose. It has, however, long been symbolic of all the enemies of idolatry. The hatred of Judaism is an aspect of modern if not all Western idolatry, that is, of the impulse arising from the horror of existence and the desire to leave the condition of the metaxy. Consider the case of Jean Paul Sartre, whose philosophy is the most recent great philosophy considered by Fackenheim.

Sartre is the outstanding figure of leftwing humanistic atheism. His antagonism to Judaism, together with his well-known sympathy for persecuted Jews, troubles Fackenheim. It may well be the case, Fackenheim thinks, that Sartre's position is the product of his view that "an individual's freedom is...destroyed by a divine Other," i.e., by God.[27] But Fackenheim does not sufficiently consider the effect the doctrine of freedom works upon Judaism. He does not consider that sympathy for persecuted Jews is a self-delusion, an indulgence sparked by little more than self-love and by the prosaic desire of even philosophic minds to be regarded as humane by the unphilosophic. As for opposition to the divine Other, it is an act of the greatest possible consequences.

Sartre's view of freedom is idolatrous. It depends on the replacement of the One with freedom. But this freedom, gnostic in form, is not theoretically stagnant. It leads somewhere. It leads to Melian exodus, that is, it permits Sartre to say that he does not know if antisemitism is "wrong or right" in socialist countries.[28] But Sartre would know if racism is wrong or right. Is this another "philosophical failure" as in Heidegger's case?

The process we find in Hitler – from self-conscious Melian exodus to an unintended gnostic exodus imposed upon him by the core of his project or the replacement of the divine with the human – we also find in Sartre. In Sartre, however, the order of exodus is reversed. Sartre's replacement of God with freedom is ultimately an assault upon theory or reason; it is the idolatry we have discovered in Hitler which does not distinguish reality from history or the struggle for power. Accordingly Sartre must ultimately look to history, as had Hegel and Marx, as the source of human reason. The individual's freedom then becomes a matter of struggle against history in the manner of neo-Kantians or Emersonians who look to the vanishing of swine and madhouses brought about by an impulse of spirit or will. But this is the same gnostic denouement into which a crude reasoner such as Hitler stumbled. Hitler is not a bastard-child of the Enlightenment, only a relatively childish enlightener. His erstwhile opponents, those who have trivialized his deeds, are less childish but not less idolatrous.

Trivialization of the Holocaust is then the failure to consider Nazism idolatrous. We have suggested that false freedom arises in connection with two continuing human impulses: to regard human being as either wholly animal or, oppositely, as godlike. In both instances the distinction between good and evil evaporates along with reality as given to a self-experiencing ego. If man is an animal, hence matter, he is subject to cause and effect; he is not responsible. If man is a god imprisoned in matter, good and evil are parts of the prison affecting his material condition only. If in the first case men cannot choose, in the second will only is free; that is, self-reliance or independence is the condition achieved with the destruction or vanishing of swine and madhouses, of reality. At the point of freedom men will know how to recognize the wisdom of Emerson's command: "*Do not choose*....Place yourself in the middle of the stream of power and wisdom which animates all whom it floats, and you are without effort impelled to truth, to right, and a perfect contentment." ("SL", CW, II, 82, 81) The familiar or naturalistic case is known to us as "relativism." Its institutional foundation is social science.

Thus the Holocaust, according to two Jewish social scientists who have studied the subject, is an example, unique in its excess, of how men mistakenly put obedience above other, better traits. Seeking a model or prototype of this human failing in Western civilization the authors hit upon the Akedah, the binding of Isaac by Abraham, his father. Their reasoning is as follows:

> [In] the Judeo-Christian tradition...wrongdoing is utterly clear....[It] is unauthorized pleasure. It is also very clear that hardly anywhere in this tradition is there any story or statement to the effect that 'Thou shalt not obey legal orders from superiors if they seem [sic?] atrocious to you.' Abraham, who was prepared to obey the directive to murder his son Isaac as a demonstration of his faith in the superior being Jaweh, is not condemned for his blind obedience, but rather held up as exemplary.[29]

It is Abraham, the first Jew and the man who defied all other men on earth in proclaiming God as the measure of all things, who is here said to be the cause of the Holocaust. Here, to be sure, is a literal trivialization of the Holocaust. Obedience to Hitler by German Nazis is counted the equivalent of obedience to God by Abraham (and Isaac). It is clear the authors, Kren and Rappoport, consider obedience to God or to Hitler the same because honest rationality calls upon social scientists to regard all objects of valuation as equal. The authors, as we say, do not believe in God. But we have already suggested the source of this atheism is not a theological investigation. It is an opinion regarding theory, or rather the supposed necessary limit upon theory imposed by the effort to insure man's freedom.

Harry Neumann has called social science of this type modern Epicureanism because it seeks tranquility of mind on the principle that "freedom from pain is man's summum bonum." If all ends are equal, if "no favoritism would be shown to any particular claim," any suggestion of superiority or of divine election constitutes an impertinence, a threat to science and peace. The equation of obedience to God and to Hitler presupposes the equality of ends.

But is not knowledge of the "superhuman vantage point" reserved to God? This is the vantage point assumed by modern Epicureans who insist that "philosophy's quest to the answer of the question of the good life is over." The good life is freedom from pain and the good is pleasure. For this reason modern Epicureans consider religion evil and threatening. Religion does not promise freedom from pain as the equivalent of the good or claim that all ends are equal. In this religion and philosophy are together the enemies of "modern Epicureanism's final solution."[30]

In saying that Abraham was a model of "blind obedience" that should be despised, Kren and Rappoport wish plainly to indict Judeo-Christian civilization as the source of the Holocaust. Above all, Judaism is the source of the Holocaust.

The case of Abraham, the first Jew and the father of Judaism, is undoubtedly pertinent to the subjects of obedience and idolatry. Abraham was the son of Terach, an idol maker. Obedient to God, he cast his father's idols into the fire. But Abraham was not a rebellious or whimsical son. Hitler and Himmler were obedient only to whim, to themselves, and they cast people into furnaces. In other words, the Nazis proceeded on the principle that Kren and Rappoport believe to be the great truth after the Holocaust, that "there is no morality per se, because there is no immutable religious or legal standard for human behavior."[31] Precisely the Nazis confounded pleasure, authorized or not, with the good. Abraham understood the good to be distinct from pleasure, from his whim, because he did not suppose he possessed divine knowledge to regard all claims as equal. In recognizing reason he recognized its source. For this reason he rejected his father's unreason or idolatry.

Abraham's obedience to God was disobedience to the atrocious rule of men. More important, Abraham defied Nimrod, the first "mighty man upon the earth...a crafty hero before God."[32] The significance of Abraham's defiance of Nimrod could not be greater for an understanding of idolatry. Nimrod is the founder of political idolatry, the first to suppress men lefneh hashem, in God's name. Nimrod claimed the superhuman vantage point as his own. Terach brought the idol-hating Abraham to Nimrod, but Abraham did not

recant. Nimrod, indulging an impulse natural to political idolators –
it was to become Hitler's trademark – cast Abraham into the fiery
furnace. But Abraham survived. Abraham is the founding symbol,
also in fire, that God and not man is the measure of all things. Like
the burning bush, Abraham becomes a sign of the One that does not
perish. But Abraham's brother, Haran, supposing Abraham's
survival demonstrated Abraham was now the new king, followed him
into the fire and, of course, he died.

Naturally Judaism survived the burning of Jews by Hitler. Hitler,
like Nimrod, was mistaken in thinking the soul is a thing. Hitler was
also mistaken in thinking man is a god who can defy the order of
being and assume the superhuman vantage point. As for the
trivialization of the Holocaust, its source is the incapacity to
distinguish the blind obedience of Haran from Abraham's
obedience. Haran, unlike Abraham, obeyed any authority
indiscriminately, because he held that there is no morality per se; he
craved unauthorized pleasure. He craved the highest pleasure in fact
or immortality.

The explanation of modern social scientists that Judaism is the
cause of the Holocaust, of Jewhatred, is exactly the explanation of
Hitler. And we have said that Judaism, and not some generalized or
universalized fear of differences, or scapegoating or any of the many
other familiar and in truth anti-Jewish explanations is the true source
of Jewhate. In other words, the basis for Jewhatred is constituted by
a love of what Judaism hates or idolatry. The convergence of Hitler's
hatred of Judaism and that of Kren and Rappoport whose stance is
one of sympathy for persecuted Jews (recall Hitler also deplored as
immoral such persecutions) is a consequence of the two aspects of
idolatry we have reviewed, namely Melian or rightwing idolatry and
gnostic or leftwing idolatry.

Emerson's claim is that each man, when he is liberated from
imprisonment by society which binds his conscience, is his own moral
authority. No doubt this amounts to a claim that there is no morality
per se. But the character of Emerson's morality, based upon man's
coming godhood, is more profound and important as a philosophical
proposal, and in its influence, than the doctrines of naturalistic

freedom characteristic of social science. Emerson's procedure, which was part of the goals he sought, was to seduce his reader. As part of this objective his exoteric or surface prose is a kind of bait.

Emerson's words, in mottos and samplers, today adorn the widow's parlour and the scholar's journal. Especially has Emerson affected the Jew. For example, Milton R. Konvitz has said, in a quintessential utterance of the Jewish liberal mind, that Emerson expresses "the genius of Judaism."[33] This sentiment, which most American Jews would be hard-pressed to dispute, helps us to understand why, in the words of Harry Neumann, "most contemporary Jews cheerfully transmit some version of modern Epicurean theology to their children. Far from experiencing it as idolatry, they praise it as modern enlightenment's victory over archaic superstition."[34]

Emerson did not express the genius of Judaism in fact. Rather Emerson expressed the genius of certain teachings deeply opposed to Judaism. That contemporary Jews, spiritual heirs of Spinoza more often than of Moses, have missed Emerson's explicitly anti-Jewish purpose is perhaps no less odd than the failure of secularist Christians to perceive it. More, it is not irrelevant to note in passing, before we consider Emerson's writings, that scholars have typically dismissed Emerson's visible "social antisemitism" as merely an expression of his times. In other words, our expectation is that Jewhatred is not to be found among such friends of mankind as Emerson – or Voltaire or Jefferson, to name only some of the most notable of this group. We are inclined to disregard antisemitic comment as aberrant when it appears, or else to charge it to the Zeitgeist. Emerson routinely identified Jews as usurers and lowminded people. "The Polish Jew," for example, Emerson pronounced animalistic and degrading although the only Polish Jew he is known to have seen was in a picture hanging in a Boston art gallery. (JMN, VII, 221–2) The remark of Emerson's daughter Ellen about the poet Emma Lazarus – that she was "a real unconverted Jew...who had no objection to calling herself one" also suggests the atmosphere of the Emerson household on the Jewish question.[35] But Emerson scholars have not been alerted by evidence of this type to consider the possibility of a wider anti-Jewish purpose because they have tended to regard statements against Jews as typical. Indeed they are, but then perhaps they have import beyond time and place.

Denying the non-historical ground of Emerson's Jewhatred as they also deny the philosophic aspect of Jewhatred generally, scholars appear to subscribe to a view of things that would in reality deny the seriousness, actually the existence, of Jewhatred altogether. Thus, the failure to see that new language, and not new attitudes, makes the Jewhatred of one time only superficially different from what has become a discredited language about Jews (which language scholars typically dismiss as having been acceptable at the time), leads inescapably to the conclusion that Jewhatred never really exists at all. In our time, for example, no scholarly or liberal person will wish to be identified by the name of antisemite, a term introduced when no scholarly or liberal person could afford to be identified with the term Jewhater. But the hatred of things Jewish is nonetheless the essence of our time, as it is the essence of scholarly and liberal morality. The new name for this hatred is "anti-Zionism." This is the conclusion of none other than Marx. Men do not hate Jews, Marx insisted; they only hate capitalism and exchange, the Jew's god.

The frank dislike of things Jewish that Emerson shared with other outstanding spokesmen for freedom in his time was not idiosyncratic. No less than in earlier times, or in later ones, men in Emerson's day were quick to discover in Judaism the final obstacle to the liberation of man as man. This opposition of Judaism and liberation in Emerson, as in Jefferson, turned upon the infallible conflict of Judaism with the modern project. For Jefferson and Emerson Jews were a cruel people whose opinions, especially Jewish morality, were reformed by Christianity. "Their ethics," said the Virginian, "are repulsive and anti-social as respecting other nations. They need reformation in an eminent degree." Especially was the Jew's God "a being of terrific character, cruel, vindictive, capricious, and unjust."[36]

Emerson's views were the same as Jefferson's. Men's "creeds" are "a disease of the intellect," ("SR", CW, II, 45) he said. Especially does this "disease of the intellect" appear to be cowardice where it is found among "those foolish Israelites." (Ibid.)

Emerson devoted his life's work to explaining what brave men do. His words sing praises to a brave man who would "read God directly," put aside his written fables and join himself to what Emerson called Nature. ("AS", CW,I,57) A man can choose divinity and in being true to his nature he can discover morality within himself. Emerson's method for becoming brave and its deep irreconcilability and hostility to Jewish life is a subject of high interest to the American historian and not only to the student of letters. The purpose of these pages will be to consider the substance of Emerson's opposition to Judaism as a central aspect of modern liberalism.

Notes

1. Eric Voegelin, *The Ecumenic Age* (Baton Rouge, 1974), 182, 181.
2. Allan Bloom, "The Study of Texts," in Melvin Richter, ed., *Political Theory and Political Education* (Princeton, 1980), 122.
3. Ibid.
4. Ibid.
5. Exodus 32:4.
6. Daniel 4:25.
7. Deuteronomy 6:4.
8. Quoted in Voegelin, *The Ecumenic Age*, 182. "Of the gods we believe, and of men we know, that by a necessity of nature they rule wherever they can. We neither made this law nor were the first to act on it; we found it to exist before us and we shall leave it to exist forever after us; we only make use of it, knowing that you and everybody else, if you were as strong as we are, would act as we do."
9. Alan Bullock, "The Political Ideas of Adolf Hitler," in Howard Fertig, ed., *The Third Reich* (New York, 1975), 352.
10. Voegelin, *The Ecumenic Age*, 182.
11. Ibid.
12. Adolf Hitler, *Mein Kampf* (New York, 1925, 1927 [1939]), 221, 442, 217, 288–289, 841, 195.
13. Adolf Hitler, Speech, 1932 cited in *Mein Kampf*, 402n6.
14. John Humphrey Noyes, *History of American Socialism* (Philadelphia, 1870, reprint edition titled, *Strange Cults and Utopias of Nineteenth Century America*, New York, 1966), vii, 626.
15. Norman O. Brown, *Life Against Death* (New York, 1961), 155.
16. Donatien A.F. de Sade, *Philosophy in the Bedroom* (Paris, 1975), in Richard Seaver and Austryn Wainhouse, eds., *The Marquis de Sade, the Complete Justine, Philosophy in the Bedroom and Other Writings* (New York, 1965), 330–331, 333.

17. Fackenheim, *Encounters*, 188.

18. Genesis 9:4,5.

19. Karl Marx, "On the Jewish Question," in T.B. Bottomore, ed., *Karl Marx: Early Writings* (New York, 1964), 37–40.

20. Hitler, *Mein Kampf*, 44.

21. Ibid., 416, 417.

22. Erich Fromm, *The Art of Loving* (New York, 1956), 15.

23. Hitler, *Mein Kampf*, 410, 102.

24. Ibid., 988.

25. Ibid., 647.

26. Adolf Hitler, Speech 26 March 1936 in N.H. Baynes, ed., *The Speeches of Adolf Hitler, April 1922–August 1939* (2 vols., New York, 1969), 2, 1317.

27. Fackenheim, *Encounters*, 209.

28. Ibid., 211.

29. George M. Kren and Leon Rappoport, *The Holocaust and the Crisis of Human Behavior* (New York, 1980), 141.

30. Harry Neumann, "Torah or Philosophy? Jewish Alternatives to Modern Epicureanism", *The Journal of Value Inquiry*, XI (1977), 17, 20.

31. Kren and Rappoport, *The Holocaust*, 142.

32. Genesis 10:8–9.

33. Milton R. Konvotz, *Judaism and the American Idea* (Ithaca, New York, 1978), 201.

34. Neumann, "Torah or Philosophy?", 24.

35. Quoted in Ralph L. Rusk, *The Life of Ralph Waldo Emerson* (New York, 1949), 494. See also JMN, VIII, 324, X, 183 and Ralph Rusk ed., *The Letters of Ralph Waldo Emerson* (6 vols.; New York, 1939), I, 227, 327.

36. Andrew A. Lipscomb and Albert E. Bergh, eds., *The Writings of Thomas Jefferson* (18 vols.; Washington, D.C., 1905), X, 382, XV, 260.

CHAPTER 3

Emerson and the Jewish Idea

Emerson's revision of Judaism (by way of a revision of Platonism to which we shall turn momentarily) was the core of his teaching. "Two ideas, Greece & Jewry, sway us," said Emerson ruefully in 1851. (JMN, XI, 402) Emerson's revision of Jewry calls at the outset for a careful study of his allied revision of Platonism. These tasks of exposition reveal Emerson's intention. It was, as Harold Bloom has justly described it, that of poet and humanist in the deepest and also in the most literal sense of both terms.

Of poetry, Bloom says "it is god-making...and [the poet]...is...as much daemon as man or woman." As for humanism, it "seeks our renewal as makers which hopes to give us the immodest hope that we – even we – coming so late in time's injustices can still sing a song of ourselves."[1] Emerson, a "strong poet" as Bloom calls those writers such as Emerson who vigorously seek "our renewal as makers," was necessarily a revisionist. "Emerson set out to excel in 'Divinity,'" writes Bloom, "by which he meant, from the start, 'eloquence.'"[2]

Emerson's revision of Greece, or what he called Plato, is embodied in a kind of Neoplatonism. Plato, said Emerson, embraced "both sides of every great question." (JMN, IX, 279) This statement, and others like it, justify the observation of an Emerson student that "few philosophers or classical scholars would be willing to admit...Plato's mind was such as...[Emerson] described it."[3]

Emerson was, in truth, no Platonist. Although at least one historian
has challenged this view, insisting that Emerson "knew well enough
what he was doing," there can be little doubt that Emerson's grasp of
Plato did not extend much beyond sentences and paragraphs which
he took for uses of his own.[4]

That Emerson was greatly interested in Plato, or in something he
saw in Plato, is plain enough, however. He turns to Plato in
Nature (1836) for no less an important object than a definition of
" 'the problem of philosophy.' " (*N*,CW,I,33) Fourteen years later in
"Plato", Emerson's first of five essays upon what he called
representative men, Emerson evaluated the Greek philosopher in
the highest possible terms. He says in that later essay that "Plato is
philosophy, and philosophy, Plato." ("P", W, IV, 40) This may seem
extravagant praise even to those who argue that Western philosophy
is a footnote to Plato. Emerson also professes a willingness to submit
to Plato's notoriously unfriendly judgment against poets. Moreover,
because Emerson's estimate of Plato is constant, extending beyond a
period that two of the more careful students of Emerson regard as a
watershed in his development – the publication of "Experience" in
1844 – one necessarily supposes that Platonism had some role in
Emerson's thought.[5] In fact, Emerson's "Plato" has an altogether
critical role in Emerson. But Emerson's reference to Plato for a
definition of philosophy in *Nature* is decisive less because of any
Platonic affinities in that essay than because of the importance of
Nature. It is widely agreed that *Nature* is the "definitive statement
of...[Emerson's] position."[6] If so, then something of substance
regarding Emerson's Platonism must be discoverable in *Nature*. One
historian, S.G. Brown, who in addition to believing that Emerson
was the purest possible type of Platonist, also does not doubt that
Nature contains "all [of Emerson's]...later thinking...[as] summary
and prophecy." Emerson, says Brown, "begins with Plato." In
particular Brown thinks the following quotation by Emerson,
appearing in *Nature*, is the polestar of his Platonism and of his
position generally. Thus: " 'The problem of philosophy,' according
to Plato, 'is, for all that exists conditionally, to find a ground
unconditioned and absolute.' "[7] We agree that this quotation is the

soul of Emerson's Platonism. It is also true that *Nature* is the summary and prophecy of Emerson's work.

Emerson's quoting of Plato reflects a truth of a kind about Emerson and his Platonism but this truth is not an obvious one and certainly it is not Platonic. There are several good reasons for saying this. The first reason is that the dictum Emerson quotes as Plato's is actually from Kant, not Plato. In fact, Emerson appears to have taken the quotation from Coleridge who himself had lifted it from Kant and then assigned it to Plato. But there is a second and related point. It is that scholars had to wait more than a century before they learned, from René Wellek, that there is, "of course, no such passage in Plato," at all.[8] Would this not suggest that our reading of Emerson has been somewhat primitive in spite of the extreme attention paid to him? Emerson was, as Bloom correctly points out, a misreader of texts. How then are we to take this important and characteristic misreading of Plato? The question has both thematic and methodological interest.

Did Emerson actually mistake a Kantian principle for Platonism? If he did, how are we to assess so apparently shocking an instance of philosophical ingenuousness, to say the very least? Or was Emerson misreading Coleridge? The possibilities are many and they are not easily resolved except for one: Emerson was no Platonist. The thematic significance of Emerson's misreading here, we may say, establishes, negatively at least, Emerson's philosophic position. As a matter of method, the misquotation assures us of Emerson's daring. He is clearly prepared to carry to the highest levels the romantic motif of the genius who casts aside every obstacle to his self-fulfillment. In sum, if Emerson's would-be Platonism informs *Nature* as the summary and prophecy of his position – a position, as we maintain, identical to the revision of "Jewry" – it is of the greatest importance to know what Emerson thought Platonism was and how Platonism as such differs from this.

Emerson's intentional misreading of texts, whether by means of a negligent disregard for the appurtenances of scholarship or by the self-conscious altering of another's words, should suggest to us what is meant by the idea that Emerson pursued divinity by means of eloquence. It should prepare us as well for the possibility that Emerson has reserved his most important misreadings for the text of texts, for the book that is called The Book, the Bible. Certainly Emerson encourages his readers to anticipate this possibility as when he writes in "Self-Reliance", in 1841, that a text is of greatest use to the reader who shall himself be a writer or, even more so, a speaker.

Emerson's hermeneutical, or, actually his antihermeneutical principle is an appropriate introduction to his Platonism because Plato possessed an opposite view of language. Too, the idea that one must find "a ground unconditioned and absolute," the Kantian quotation, contains the aspect of antiPlatonic ontology so important to Emerson's purpose. Emerson's notorious contempt for conventions, for consistency, indeed for society, that "conspiracy against...manhood," was not only a device calculated to win applause from intellectuals who prize non-conformity on principle. ("SR", CW, II, 29) Emerson's impulse went much deeper, indeed to "god-making." We are led by Emerson's misreading of Plato to consider the contrast between Plato and Emerson, a contrast pertinent to Emerson's intentional misreading of Judaism.

Although Emerson is frequently classed among Platonists or at least as part of a Neoplatonic tradition, the two are not the same. Emerson assumed the persona of Plato, not his ideas. This is a fact of importance. Emerson, in other words, was eager to take on the authority of Plato's name but solely for the sake of promoting Emersonian principles. His use of Plato in *Nature* attests to a rather literal application of this approach. In order to judge the extent of Emerson's deviation from Plato it is helpful to compare Emerson's use of Plato with Plato's use of Socrates. Socrates speaks for himself and there is a Platonic reason for this – Plato shuns "definitions" of philosophy. Speech of this type, as we know from the Seventh Epistle particularly, as well as from the entire Platonic oeuvre, is regarded by Plato as lying beyond language. Moreover, Socrates, as a Platonic speaker, speaks for others – for example, for the sophist Protagoras, at just those times when Plato wishes to expose the grave dangers to philosophy that accompany attempts, as by Protagoras, to "define" philosophy. Is it not indeed in Protagoras, as imitated by

Socrates, that Emerson is found? Socrates, speaking as Protagoras, argues that a true teacher "is not...a man...[who] makes someone who previously thought what is false think what is true, for it is not possible...to think...anything but what one experiences, and all experiences are true...[Therefore] one set of thoughts is better than the other but not in any way truer."[9]

Here is Emerson's argument for "an original relation to the universe," for his ideal of the human self that emerges when liberated from "society," from nature and the past, above all, from "all mean egotism." (*N*, CW, I, 10) " 'I neither am going nor coming; nor is my dwelling in any one place; nor art thou, thou; nor are others, others; nor am I, I' " ("P", W, IV, 50). But this description of the self, inserted by Emerson in his essay "Plato", is again Protagorean. Socrates says, speaking once more as Protagoras, that a person is not "one person at all [even when considered distinct but] several, indeed an infinite succession of persons."[10] When Emerson describes Plato as one who "could argue on this side and on that...[so that no one] could even tell what Platonism was," he describes himself, or rather he describes Protagoras as conceived by Plato's ironic muse ("P", W, IV, 78). This description reveals Emerson's inversion of Plato's conception of the one and the many. This inversion, a product of Emerson's use of language, introduces the essential element of Emerson's outward or philosophic position.

Emerson's belief that Plato embraced both sides of every question is a reordering of the one and the many as Plato understood these terms. Emerson wrote in "Plato" that Plato apprehended the cardinal facts that "lie forever at the base, the one, and the two, – 1. Unity, or Identity; and 2. Variety. We unite all things by perceiving the law which pervades them; by perceiving the superficial differences and the profound resemblances....It is impossible to speak or to think without embracing both." ("P", W, IV, 47–8) Emerson, literally identifying language and thinking, identifies both with speaking. But is it not exactly Plato's point that such an identification is eristical, even nonsense? Such an identification is meant to show the power of the will in controlling or creating reality. But this is what men must resist, according to Plato, as the highest expression of irrationality. Thus while the "combination," of the one and the two, as Emerson says, "is obvious," it is the reverse of Platonic.

Of course Plato did not suppose that being could be defined, its parts listed conveniently for student note-taking. Plato sought ways to shield his discoveries from abuses of this type. What he did suggest, drawing upon the theoretical terminology of his predecessors, was a kind of ontological geography in *Philebus*. Plato conceived being in four modes: the Unlimited or apeiron; the limited; mixture or metaxy; and cause (aitia) or One. This conception of Plato's is a differentiation of the ontology of Anaximander conceived two centuries earlier. The Ionian called "the origin...of things...the Apeiron....It is necessary," he said "for things to perish into that from which they were born; for they pay one another penalty for their injustice according to the ordinance of time."[11] But it is the discovery of the consciousness of the process, that is, of reason, that is most important. It is the Platonic, or generally, the classical idea of reason as the site of transcendence that separates modern civilization from that of Plato. Our modern supposition is that reason in man is an adaptive mechanism differing only in degree from similar mechanisms in other animals. Language, accordingly, has taken on most remarkable meanings – some of which we shall consider – in modern times and in thinkers such as Emerson. But the Platonic conception of reason as distinguishing man from gods and beasts also involves a most unEmersonian concept of language.

Reason, writes the German scholar of Platonism Paul Friedlander, is "the cause that masters the limitless by means of the limit."[12] Reason partakes of the One or, as Aristotle said, it is "moved" by it. Thus is the apeirontic, or Unlimited, limited. This limit is Plato's form. This is to say that Plato's famous *ideas* are not, as students seem nowadays to be taught, some heavenly statuary or "absolutes" unconditioned as a ground of the conditioned. The ideas or forms are the order of reality and the means to order human affairs. They are known only to man among the creatures that partake of the apeiron or that perish.

Man is then in between the apeirontic and the One. This condition of existence is the metaxy. This is the relation that Emerson wanted to revise. He wanted to obliterate the in between. This is no abstruse, merely academic matter though we owe our inclination to dismiss it as such to the destruction of the philosophic by academics who instruct students to believe that philosophy is historical and relative at best, and at worst, as in the thought of Marx or Dewey, an obstacle to revolutionary and liberating action. Philosophy as the love of wisdom rejects on principle or we may even say on faith the two alternatives which are not philosophic; the claim either that man is all matter or that he is spirit momentarily imprisoned in matter. In other words, the necessary condition of philosophy is a commitment to man's position in between beasts and the divine: Plato's "position." This too is the commitment of Judaism or of any religion that is not idolatrous. The in-between condition (the Torah in Judaism and the incarnation in Christianity), is the realm of monotheism. Yet Emerson's aspiration is that the apeirontic should be one; in particular, the one that is man. Emerson differentiates man's soul from the apeirontic, identifying it with what is the divine Nous in Plato. He substitutes the Unlimited for the Limit; instinct, or making for reason or theory. Let us consider this in Platonic terms.

The Anaximanderian discovery to which Plato has recourse in *Philebus* was of two modes of being; apeiron as the origin, as the Unlimited ground of all things, and apeiron as the things themselves which are limited by time, hence perishable. Man participates in both modes insofar as he is a thing with access to the whole. Plato, and later Aristotle, unpacked or differentiated this truth of Anaximander. Plato discerned in the apeiron or Unlimited a limit as we have seen. Specifically Plato found the principle of the limit or consciousness of the process in man's desire to know. Voegelin has described this as the discovery of "man's consciousness as the area of reality in which the process of reality becomes luminous to itself."[13] This Platonic limit is man's search of the ground which is present in the apeiron as Origin. Moreover, this origin, or divine Nous, is also limited by the apeirontic forces, by flux or necessity (Ananke) in which it and the search of the ground exist. But the human nous, hence also the search of the ground (the process of reasoning or noesis), is itself the expression of limit in that it measures, limits, and molds the apeirontic. The nous is then that which orders. This is what is meant by the claim that man, so far as he reasons, partakes of something that is not the apeiron but rather of the origin; of the divine. Not all political philosophers in our time have rejected this discovery or the language in which it was first conveyed. For example, Leo Strauss has said that "the human soul is the only part of the whole which is open to the whole and therefore more akin to the whole than anything else is."[14] Eric Voegelin has likewise not relinquished the classical vantage point. His synopsis of the Platonic modes of being is pertinent.

> Plato symbolizes the mystery of being as existence between the poles of the One...and the unlimited (apeiron). Where the One changes over into the many...and the Unlimited into the Limited, there arises, between the two poles, the number and form of 'things.' This area of form and number is the In-Between (Metaxy) of the One...and the Unlimited....The metaxy is the domain of human knowledge.[15]

We stress here that Plato's concept of limit or reason is not confined to Plato or to any system. It belongs instead to all of non-modernist noesis excepting the (until recent years) minor philosophic tradition stemming from Epicurus. In this sense it is perhaps correct to say philosophy is a footnote to Plato and, in saying so, to gauge the difference between Plato and Emerson's Plato. In this connection, we may usefully compare the Platonic and Emersonian idea of philosophy. Leo Strauss has explained philosophy as the operation of Platonic reason. Thus philosophy, although it

> strives for knowledge of the whole...[the knowledge we actually possess is necessarily partial. It is] characterized by a fundamental dualism which has never been overcome. At one pole we find knowledge of homogeneity...arithmetic....At the opposite pole we find knowledge of heterogeneity, and in particular of heterogeneous ends....It seems that knowledge of the whole would have to combine somehow political knowledge in the highest sense with knowledge of homogeneity. And this combination is not at our disposal.[16]

The philosopher is the one who balances and who is balanced. His knowledge, informed by the One, is not itself One. And yet the philosopher's knowledge, although partial, is not apeirontic; it is not absolute in any sense. The philosopher's knowledge is theoretical and proceeds by theory, theory being that which is neither One or apeirontic, but a mixture of these. Theory is not a thing, or a making, but the divine means by which search of the ground takes place. Moreover, it is important that we understand the Platonic method for achieving this in-between condition. Not only does this method differ from the Cartesian method, emphasizing "science," and from the so-called humanist approach or what Strauss calls the delusion of "humble awe," it marks with great clarity the opposition between Emersonian methods and Platonic ones.[17] The first point of difference then between philosophy in the Platonic mode and Emersonian philosophy is in the area of so-called methods.

Plato's method, the means by which the metaxy is reached and the noetic process carried on, is the erotic method. The importance of eros in Plato, and its absence or rather its hypostatization as "love" in Emerson, is one of several indices to Emerson's transformation of Platonic symbols, hence to Emerson's revision of the Platonic ontological modes. Eros in the soul is not unrelated to physical love. Nevertheless eros is opposed to physical love. The connection of eros to religious subjects (for which *The Song of Songs* is the *locus classicus*) reflects a high order of philosophic intensity. The Platonic dialogue is itself perhaps the best philosophic demonstration of what is meant by eros.

In the study of texts, especially those such as Emerson's wherein a Platonic persona hides a Protagorean purpose as in the example we cited earlier, it becomes a matter of first importance to comprehend the erotic intention. This intention is rooted in our common perception of physical beauty. But physical beauty ironically enough is only a metaphor or symbol of imperishable elements – symmetry, form, limit, control – that make up perishable and sensible beauty. But eros in the soul signals our release from the dominion of physical eros, enemy of the soul's liberty; of its symmetry, form, limit and control. And this liberty is not only liberty from sex but from death or thanatos as well. Recall that it was Orpheus who redeemed souls from death in the Greek legend. Orpheus redeemed Eurydice, the mate of his couch, but lost her again when he could not resist the temptation to turn his gaze hellward for a glimpse of her beauty. The contrast between Platonic eros and Emersonian eros, between liberation from death or the apeirontic on one side, and liberation toward the apeirontic by means of the apeirontic and the sexual on the other side, indicates the difference between Emerson and Plato. It is no accident that Emerson's "Orphic poet," in *Nature*, is the one to speak for Emerson's dream of man as god.

In Plato liberation from death and the fear of death, liberation, that is to say, from the apeirontic, is made possible by eros; love for that level of being (the One) which is not the apeirontic but what Plato calls Agathon or the Good. We are no doubt familiar with Platonic eros in our time by its reversal, that is, by the depreciation of reason. The modern inversion of eros which promises liberation by means of an apeirontic embrace of death, violence, and sex, reflects exactly a hatred of limit, symmetry, and form. It is this reversal that Emerson's life work endows. The difference between the Platonic and the Emersonian eros emerges from a comparison of the pronouncements of Emerson's oracular advisor, the Orphic poet of *Nature* just mentioned, and the advice Diotima gave to the youthful Socrates.

Plato tells us in the *Symposium*, the subject of which is love, that Socrates consulted the oracle as a youth. What Diotima teaches, says Socrates, is that eros is not a god. Love is of the in between, of the metaxy. And, Plato insinuates, Socrates followed the teaching of Diotima, becoming a great lover, specifically a lover of what eros is not, of what the metaxy is not: a lover of the One ("Good" or "Beauty"). Love for the Good is a direction. This implies an end or telos. But the lover, Socrates, pursues the Good. He does not possess it. He does not suppose his loving is the Good; that "God is love." Loving does not constitute the Good. Socrates is not the Good or at one with the Good. Eros is a lacking that seeks what it is not. There is no love as such, as there is no speech as such. Socrates' love is balanced. It abides by the consideration of existence revealed to him and to common sense by the facts of existence. He does not resist existence by aspiring to divinity. He has no wish to make reality disappear so that he can build his own world, the project that Emerson recommends to all men in the concluding section of *Nature*. How different is Socrates' worship of the Diotima from Emerson's of his Orphic poet.

Nature is Emerson's longest prose work. In the last of eight sections called "chapters" that make up *Nature*, Emerson invokes "a certain poet...my Orphic poet." (*N*, CW, I, 41, 42) This poet is Emerson, although the poet's comments are quoted as if taken from another source. Emerson's exaggerated deference to scholarly standards, actually to the integrity of another's word, is of course ironic, standing as it does in juxtaposition to his earlier quotation from Kant in Plato's name. The Orphic poet speaks twice, his last speech concluding the essay with a famous sentence: " 'The kingdom of man over nature, which cometh not with observation, – a dominion such as now is beyond his dream of God, – he shall enter without more wonder than the blind man feels who is gradually restored to perfect sight.' " (Ibid., 45) The Orphic poet commends a most complete freedom: *viz.*, the freedom to create " 'your own world.' " (Ibid.) And who but God creates worlds; how but with words are worlds to be created? In truth, the theme of *Nature* is not nature at all but dominion over it, a putting of nature "under foot" so that it shall become "the double of the man." (Ibid., 25) The Orphic poet, who is after all only Emerson himself, tells Emerson to be God. As Orpheus was the son of God, of Apollo, so is Emerson here the son of Orpheus by the only available means at hand: self-creation by means of words. Emerson's work is a celebration of Orphic power, of Emerson's power. It is a celebration of self, but what is the self or ego that Emerson has in mind? Man Thinking who rises above "all mean egotism" is an unexpected self indeed. This new man is somehow divine.

The Orphic poet confides to Emerson that man is a "god," but a god that is momentarily in ruins. This ruined man is equal to only "half his force." (Ibid., 42) But what does man fail to do? Appealing first of all to the deep strain of romanticism in contemporary and subsequent auditors, Emerson makes a prelusive and superficial answer. He says that man fails to develop his most human side favoring instead a mere technological mastery over nature. Yet this more human side, the key to divinity, is nothing less than man's "other half," and this, says Emerson, is the product of speech. When whole man or what Emerson soon comes to describe as Man Thinking is liberated into the precincts of his own world by speech, then will reality answer to a man's desires "beyond his dream of God." At that point men will discover that the real world shall be "found in combination with the human will." (Ibid., 15) We are not surprised to learn that "love" is the soul's instrument for man's acquisition of his new world. The "soul...appropriate[s] all things...by love." ("CM", CW, II, 72) Emersonian love is no kin to Plato's eros, however. On the contrary, Emerson's love opposes all limits. The "soul refuses limits." (Ibid., 71) Emerson's loving is not a lack that searches in the philosopher's mode for the always elusive whole. The eros Emerson speaks of is the whole itself. Emerson's love is gnosis; absolute knowledge embodied in the protean or selfless self. "The whole is here, – the wealth of the Universe is for me. Every thing is explicable & practicable for me." (JMN, VIII, 228) What are this soul's rewards?

The reward is a certain fatal or involuntary perception, in particular, the perception of "absolute truth." ("AS", CW, I, 56) In fact, the reward is freedom, absolute independence. This is both the essence of license or whim as well its opposite or fatality. What sense does this make? The paradoxical aspect in Emerson has delighted and frustrated his readers, some of whom have supposed that Emerson was either pulled between idealistic and pragmatic poles or else, perhaps, that he combined the idealistic and the pragmatic, whether out of perversity, confusion, or ingenuousness. But Emerson's paradoxical views, of which his vision of the self as neither an I nor a thou is the centerpiece, are self-conscious doctrine. Actually, the paradoxical aspects compose a unity in two senses. First, the oppositions of pragmatism as a would-be naturalism and idealism are seeming oppositions only. Pragmatic ontology, a neo-Kantian derivative, is radically idealistic in its aspiration to make reality accord with human needs or ideas. Secondly, the source of the theoretical unification of Emersonian paradoxes is his revision, in truth his inversion, of the Platonic One. Unity is the apeirontic cast by Emerson into the role of the One; or, as he put it, the "doctrine ever new and sublime; that there is One Man." ("AS", CW, I, 53)

This is the unity that Emerson considers to be established by word-making, and thus the unity or One he envisages is the product of human making. Accordingly, the objects of reality are words. The soul, Man Thinking, partakes of this reality as does everything else; *viz.*, "the sense of being...is not diverse from things...but one with them, and...from the same source." ("SR", CW, II, 37) The apeirontic (origin and things), including time and perishing, all of which Plato assigned to the Unlimited, assumes in Emerson the position of Limit or Ideal. This is to say that the apeiron is hypostatized. Naturally good and evil, as well as death are transcended. We may note in passing the source of Nietzsche's interest in Emerson, as well as an Emersonian insinuation of "eternal recurrence." The one and the many are unified because time and the elements of the apeiron are hypostatized or absolutized. "Every thing has two sides, a good and an evil." ("CM", CW, II, 70) Emerson calls this compensation.

In giving his reason for writing the essay "Compensation", Emerson said he considered it in part a corrective to the views of a "preacher...esteemed for...orthodoxy," who made the reward of virtue the permission to sin in the hereafter. (Ibid., 55) This view, no orthodox one by the way, is Emersonian in at least the degree that it emphasized compensation. It is the preacher's idea of virtue and reward in the hereafter that Emerson disputes. Having dispensed with "the antique and future worlds" and also with memory, all compensation, like the whole, is "here for me" in the eternal present. Emerson says that good and evil apply to all things. Thought, of course, is one of these things. Emerson's paradox, his relativism and its absolute or timeless form, takes its rise from the timeless present, the *nunc stans*. Likewise, his vision of a free or liberated ego, absolutely self-reliant at the same time that it is merged with all other egos, is a product of timeless time, Emerson's new world. The pragmatic character of thought, its realization in action, is Emerson's instrument (he does not, that is, make history as matter or idea his instrument) for the resolution of the paradoxes to which he incessantly gives birth.

Thought is a making or an acting which like all Emersonian things comes into being and perishes according to the ordinance of time. But of course it is evident that Emerson's formula is the opposite of Anaximander's, time being necessarily infinite for Emerson. Compensation – the preacher's hereafter – is of this world. Just as God "re-appears with all his parts in every moss and cobweb," thought is integrated or compensated over time so that it, like God, is a whole, thus absolute. ("CM", CW, II, 60) The apeiron (things and time) have been absolutized or made infinite. But there is one "thing" which simply is, "to wit...the soul." (Ibid., 70) It does not have two sides but is one. This soul of Man Thinking is a self that has, consistently enough, neither an I nor a thou or is it in this place or in that place. Rather the soul is "many" or all. "There is One Man....He is all." ("AS", CW, I, 53) Again necessarily, the perceptions of this one man cannot be individualized or "whimsical," but instead they are fatal and involuntary. Finally, the eye of the poet must be transparent, all nature being "put...forth" through him, just as his eye must be the eye of mankind. (N, CW, I, 38) If man's perceptions, in his condition of oneness, or self-reliance, are "fatal," man's I is his eye. Man Thinking "is the world's eye." ("AS", CW, I, 62)

Bloom's view that "Emerson set out to excel in 'Divinity,'" is well-founded. Excellence in divinity, or the god-making of self by means of the "fire" of speech was plainly Emerson's object. The ancient rabbis spoke of the white fire of parchment and the black fire of words that make up the Torah. When the martyred Rabbi Hananya of Teradyon was burning alive on a pyre of Torah parchments, his grieving disciples asked him what he saw in his last moments. He told them that he saw the parchment burning, but he said the words of Torah were released by fire from the page, they escaped and rose toward heaven. Precisely this power of words is the one Emerson coveted as excellence in divinity.

Notes

1. Harold Bloom, *Figures of Capable Imagination* (New York, 1976), 55, 57.

2. Harold Bloom, "The Freshness of Transformation or Emerson on Influence," in Leonard Nick Neufeldt, ed., *Ralph Waldo Emerson; New Appraisals: A Symposium* (Hartford, Connecticut, 1973), 59.

3. Frederic Ives Carpenter, *Emerson and Asia* (New York, 1968 [1930]), 15.

4. Stuart Gerry Brown, "Emerson's Platonism," *New England Quarterly*, XVIII (1945), 327.

5. Stephen E. Whicher, *Freedom and Fate; An Inner Life of Ralph Waldo Emerson* (Philadelphia, 1953), 111ff; Bloom, *Figures of Capable Imagination*, 73.

6. Murray G. Murphey and Elizabeth Flower, *A History of Philosophy in America* (2 vols.; New York, 1977), I, 409.

7. Brown, "Emerson's Platonism," 335.

8. René Wellek, "Emerson and German Philosophy," *New England Quarterly*, XVI (1943), 54.

9. Plato, *Theaetetus*, 167a5–63.

10. Ibid., 166b5.

11. Diels, many translations. See Kathleen Freeman, *Ancilla to the Pre-Socratic Philosophers* (Cambridge, 1956), 19.

12. Paul Friedlander, *Plato* (3 vols.; Princeton, 1969), III, 328.

13. Eric Voegelin, *The Ecumenic Age* (Baton Rouge, 1974), 177.

14. Leo Strauss, "What is Political Philosophy?" in *What is Political Philosophy?* (Glencoe, Illinois, 1959), 39.

15. Voegelin, *The Ecumenic Age*, 184.

16. Strauss, "What is Political Philosophy?," 39.

17. Ibid., 40.

54

CHAPTER 4

Emerson's Freedom

Ralph Rusk, Emerson's biographer, does not overstate the case in the matter of Emerson's fascination with speaking when he notes how "deeply...the idea of the power of the orator [had] taken hold of him."[1] The speaker, said Emerson, "should have his audience at his devotion and all other fames would hush before his." (JMN, IX, 71) Thus the orator, vibrating with "throbs and heart beatings at the door of the assembly" hopes to invest his speech with world-making eloquence, "that the thought may be ejaculated as Logos or Word." (Ibid., 72) Emerson's writings are alive with words that must be realized. "Words are things," Emerson says. They "bleed." ("MS",W,IV,168)[2] Words fill the world, are the world in fact: the "abyss [shall] be vocal with speech." ("AS", CW, I, 59) In all of this Emerson proposes that man shall know only what he makes. In sum, man has no end but the ends he gives to himself.

Emerson answers the cosmological question by supposing that the cosmos is radically incomprehensible, this making all things relative. And this is his warrant for making his own world. It shall of course be perfect and absolute. Here then is the second vital difference between philosophy in Emerson's mode and Platonic philosophy. Knowledge of man-made reality, an absolute knowledge obviously since man makes it, takes the place of teleology. Emerson's claim that "disagreeable appearances, swine, spiders, snakes...madhouses...[will]...vanish...as fast as you conform your life to the pure idea in your mind," is not so poetic or otherworldly as Emerson's caricaturist friend Christopher Cranch supposed. (*N*, CW, I, 45) Emerson really meant what he said.

Emerson's dominating concern for words and for the divining power of poets, or Man Thinking, affects all aspects of his thinking. The reality of words supplies the controlling methodological theme of his work. Consider, to begin, Emerson's definition of philosophy. Looking beyond his citation of Kant as Plato in *Nature*, and his more analytical commentaries in "Plato," his understanding of philosophy reflects his rudimentary confusion, actually reversal, of the relationship of words and reality. The first thing one learns about Emerson's philosophy is that it is a revision of philosophy as Plato or the classics conceived it. By philosophy, Emerson understood what the ancients counted as myth. "Philosophy," said Emerson, "is the account which the human mind gives to itself of the constitution of the world." ("P", W, IV, 47) This confusion of the describing of the events of noesis with noesis is a further index to the character of Emerson's Platonism.

Philosophy on the classical view is not what Emerson describes. It is not the mind's discourse with itself about the world, but about the world including the mind. Philosophy is about mind and world as "problem." In other words, "to articulate the problem of cosmology means to answer the question of what philosophy is or what a philosopher is."[4] Emerson, on the contrary, would invent the "mystical" event which is the Platonic noetic openness toward the ground. To await this event may require limitation upon the poet's creativity in preference to the activity in which the waiting philosopher participates. Pertinent here, as elsewhere, is Bloom's observation that "Emerson had not the patience to wait for mysticism," mysticism itself being the impatience of those unwilling to wait for God.[5] This substituting of myth for philosophy, of the story of the search for the search, uncovers only the smallest part of the inversion and irony that lies beneath Emerson's vocabulary. Closed against the questioning of the ground, the movements "hither and thither...[in] the unobscured openness toward reality...in order to participate through distinguishing knowledge...in the structures of reality...," Emerson delights to assume the aspect of " 'liberating god' whose inspired utterances strike off the chains of tradition and convention that bind men's minds."[6] But the dialectical self or the ego that is all in one blocks out the ground. Emerson's inspired utterances would bind men's minds exactly because he would liberate them from all traditions and conventions; more precisely, he would liberate men, as he says, from the tyranny of memory.[7]

For Emerson, the whole is eclipsed by the "bipolar Unity" imposed upon the world by the self. (JMN, VII, 200) Because "the world...[is the] shadow of the soul or *other me*," it follows that the "self is the sole subject we study and learn." Furthermore, completing a circle (Emerson's favorite image of which more will be said later), the self is the world. Quite literally, it is the "Kingdom of God...within you." (JMN, III, 144; cf. Luke 17:21) But Bloom, admonishing those who, he says, want "not to see [that Emerson] is a dialectician of the spirit...who called himself a seer of unity but cheerfully enough realized he mostly beheld diversity, particulars never to be subdued," is unmindful of what a dialectic of the spirit is.[8] Is Emerson's dialectic, which discovers the world to be the "other me," two or diversity or is it one? Emerson is unquestionably a dialectician of the spirit and because he is the dualism he perceives is self or one. Emerson confessed this. Bloom is wrong here. "If...the world is not a dualism, is not a bipolar Unity, but is *two*, is Me and It, then is there the Alien, the Unknown, and all we have believed & chanted out of our deep instinctive hope is a pretty dream." (JMN, VII, 200) This is the hope, no pretty dream to philosophers, that prompts "prophetic humanists," such as Bloom and Emerson, to regard the "soul" as that which simply is. The soul stands outside "compensation" or "bipolar unity," or rather this unity stands within the soul's compass. But necessarily the price of this godly power of the soul and its encompassing of experience is high: the soul, cut off from openness to the whole, abandons the search of the ground in favor of a delectation of self. Modern Emersonians similarly forfeit knowledge about the whole, thus forfeit the human soul, for knowledge of "the workings of human language and human thought." Also like Emerson they uncover in "the intrinsic principle of mind...the object of our awe."[9] Denial of the whole, what Voegelin refers to as the prohibition of questioning, is called by Emersonians precisely openness, tolerance, freedom. That troubling and to many confusing modern identification of freedom with animal impulse or what the classical world called slavery is part of an inversion and reversal of ideals and principles at the heart of which lie such visions of self as Emerson's.

Emerson substitutes the description of philosophical events for openness to the objects of philosophy proper. This renders words, the instruments of description available to philosophy, useless for philosophic purposes. But this has the result of distorting the instruments of words, that is, metaphor, simile and the like, in ways that clarify how inadequate words are to the challenge Emerson hoped they would meet. While in philosophy words are descriptions of concepts, reality being indefinable, the changing of philosophy's object from reality to descriptions of it, to words, transforms words into concepts and reality at once, two things words are not. The ontological implausibility of this situation, visible in Emerson's many ungainly images – so ungainly as to inspire the friendly Cranch to poke fun at Emerson – is that the objects of Emerson's second reality – poet and words or the hypostatized apeiron – must stand for the indefinable as if they were reality. The practical result can only be a kind of fanatical action or misperception of events in the real world.

As a literary matter, this denial of reality on principle results in bizarre diction and usage. Metaphor, for example, grows abstract as it seeks words for words. Description likewise becomes excessively naturalistic as one attempts to bring life to words by using the words of life. This is a source of so-called realism or the literature of dirty words. It should also be evident that the realm of myth or extended metaphor is narrowed by Emerson's philosophy. What the biographer of Christopher Pearse Cranch called Emerson's "unusual diction," is traceable to Emerson's limitation of reality to words and to the poet's experience.[10] Emerson's images are so often peculiar because the world they account for is so greatly limited. Since the poet obviously cannot be in the words he writes anymore than realities can be in concepts about them, the poet is forced to press beyond capacity the ability of words to paint, even "in fire," his experience. The drawings of Cranch are inspired by this fact. Some consideration of these drawings will illustrate the points made here.

Christopher Cranch, although a Transcendentalist and an admirer of Emerson, was enough of a Yankee to question the plausibility of Emerson's more remarkable images. The humor of Cranch's drawings arises from his transfer of Emerson's metaphors and similes into the quotidian settings they violate. Consider Cranch's famous caricature of Emerson's "transparent eyeball." Cranch draws a towering stalk-like figure standing in a field with an outsized head and shocking eyeball that seems neither to see or look. Emerson's wish to "expand and live in the warm day like corn and melons" provoked the ground-hugging Cranch to draw a poet in the shape of a fat melon. Its face wears the sheepish smile of a man who has begun to have second thoughts about the propriety of sitting in a field with large leaves growing out of his head. Finally there is Cranch's response to Emerson's project for building new worlds by making swine, madhouses and other unpleasant things "vanish." And so Cranch shows us the poet who commands the cleansing of reality as he sits patiently watching madhouses, swine, snakes and pests running off the page on human legs. The absurdity is highlighted by the sight of the poet who watches this weird exodus as if it were a normal occurrence.

When Kafka's narrators speak as bugs or apes, Kafka's purpose is to excite a sense of absurdity and the grotesque. Emerson's images, milder than Kafka's, are more provocative but less useful because they assault reality for the purpose of correcting it rather than our views of it. Emerson's object is the reverse of Kafka's. Kafka prized common sense which he served in his use of the bizarre. Emerson's images are not successful because the lesson he teaches runs aground on ordinary experience. When he instructs his reader to get a new look at a familiar landscape by turning upside down to see it through his legs, this being Emerson's idea of the relativity of things, we are struck only by the banality of Emerson's observation. (*N*, CW, I, 31) The Pickwickian philosophical-experimenter, like the melon poet, is an unedifying spectacle. It is a measure of our culture or rather of the authority of our intellectual culture that the impulse to laugh, as Cranch did, at Emerson's diction, like the impulse to laugh at large segments of modern art, has been stifled.

Emerson's substitution of the objects of myth for those of philosophy includes the substitution of mythmaker or poet for philosopher. Emerson's self-conscious pursuit of the "whole man," what he calls Man Thinking, for which the model is the balanced soul of Plato, is, like the Platonic pursuit, an erotic one. But where Plato's eros is the daimon that represents the in between in search of the One, Emerson's poetic imagery is carnal. Although Emerson regards the soul as the only existing thing that is uncompensated – that is, as the One, or as it were, God, it was inescapable that his symbolism would betray the earthly origins of the Emersonian soul.

Emerson's philosophic muse not his poetic one made it inevitable that he would symbolize the soul as a combination of the two essential apeirontic entities, man and woman, melted into one. Emerson's "balanced soul" is the hermaphrodite. Cranch missed a chance here, but Plato, as we see in a moment, made fun of this caricature of eros long before Emerson took it seriously. This "unity" of man and woman, says Emerson, is the symbol of "the finished soul." (JMN, VIII, 380) Like the self or I that becomes independent when it is not I, man who is "never a man" in his "*divided* or social state," becomes a man when he embodies both man and woman; when he is not one or the other but one as both. ("AS", CW, I, 53)

Once again the intent of Emerson's symbolism is highlighted in contrast with Plato's. Emerson's hermaphrodite vision, his apeirontic and gnostic vision of the finished soul, may actually have been drawn from Plato. Emerson says he read the *Symposium* only two years before writing his comment on the finished soul in his journal in 1843. But here, once more, it is not Plato that Emerson follows but a Platonic caricature of the comic poet Aristophanes as drawn by Plato's ironic muse. Aristophanes set down a theory of love that is rooted in apeirontic unity. Consider Aristophanes' theory of love's perfected soul. He says that the model of love is physical oneness.

The ontological grotesqueness of this idea, that is, of the idea that the limitless is equivalent to the One, that the perishable is the same as the imperishable thus of the limit, is insinuated by the figure of Aristophanes himself.

Aristophanes' speech is awkward; it is out of order. Having missed his appointed time for speaking because of the hiccups (brought upon him by a recent "soaking" or drunkenness), he now prefaces his remarks about love with the hope that what he says will not be considered "utterly absurd."[11] Here Plato seems to pay back the real Aristophanes for having made a fool of Socrates in his drama *The Clouds* where Socrates appears as an utterly absurd and perfect sophist. Now the Platonic Aristophanes, a belching poet trying to be a philosopher, asks the members of the symposium or banquet to indulge his own efforts as a philosopher. Plato has cast Aristophanes in the role of that bohemian poetic type of soul who wards off the philosophic (and who is therefore an ally of the sophist) with ridicule by lumping the philosopher and the sophist together. But Plato who has written this script for Aristophanes intends to reveal Aristophanes' sophistical purpose. Aristophanes, his apologies out of the way, goes on to describe "the real nature of man." He explains:

> The race was [once] divided into three; that is to say, besides the two sexes...there was a third which partook of the nature of both, and for which we still have a name, though the creature itself is forgotten. For though 'hermaphrodite' is only used nowadays as a term of contempt, there really was a man-woman in those days....[All three, man-man, man-woman, woman-woman, were each one.][12]

Something of the dignity of man in his ancient form is suggested by the ambulatory habits of these "beings...globular in shape" who went "whirling round and round like a clown turning cartwheels. And since they had eight legs, if you count their arms...they went bowling along at a pretty good speed."[13] This entirely absurd vision of the sensual antiphilosopher is a caricature of Plato's eros. The Platonic eros seeks the Good or the One. Aristophanes' One as the biological joining of physical beings – Man as One – seems less to "complete" any meaning of Plato's than to ridicule it.[14]

Emerson's philosophic understanding with its roots in the transforming authority of words, thus in the authority of the mythmaker or poet who holds "the keys of power," is an understanding of the One as Man. (N, CW, I, 21) Plainly, knowledge arises from making. And what knowledge makes, as Emerson proclaims so frequently, is man. Emerson's conception of nature is that Man Thinking creates it. In other words, creation of nature is freedom. Freedom is the end to which all Emerson's efforts tend. It is in truth the heart of Emerson's project. Freedom is a man's release and liberation from the influence of society (which Emerson calls the past or history including memory) and books. Freedom is likened by Emerson to "unhandselled savage nature." ("AS", CW, I, 61) Its ways, surprisingly enough it seems (for do we not associate freedom with choosing and not with desiring and raw will?), are those of "instinct." Freedom is then a law of nature in which the good is the Epicurean expression of creative impulses in which every man's good is the creation of "his own world." Man has a nature only insofar as he expresses his singular constitution and thus demonstrates that man has no specific nature or that he is free. Emerson is the *artiste* whose transcendence of society by means of freedom entitles him to be the conscience of society. Thus, freedom is Emerson's "fixed point." A dialectical point, it is fixed as a "circle on a sphere." (N, CW, I, 28)

Emerson, who explicitly denies that nature is separate from man but is instead man's double, the product of his realized will or freedom, and who also maintains that justice and beauty are creation as such, does not distinguish what is good simply from what is good according to a man's constitution. He does not distinguish the good from the pleasant. Emerson's individual "does not do good," Caponigri notes, rather "he becomes good."[15] Because Emerson's conception of nature is both transhistorical and each individual's contingency, it follows that Emerson must reject social life as "unnatural." This is perhaps an essential expression of what the modern understands or fails to understand by freedom. The paradoxes or contradictions of the modern idealist who simultaneously pursues collectivist and anarchist goals will find in Emerson's idea of self-reliance a most powerful support. This would be Emerson's ideal of Man Thinking. Man Thinking is first of all a critic of social conventions, the heroic great-hearted man of Enlightenment literature and thought. Man Thinking is not a "conformist." Emerson's resounding attacks upon the idea of politics and upon the artificiality of society generally are among his most famous themes. Who can resist them? Is not a great heart infinitely superior to the crabbed ways of conformist souls? For Emerson, then, there can be no good or bad political order and hence no virtue apart from creativity because society and government are not according to nature; they are not lawful. What is lawful and natural is what is "after my constitution." ("SR", CW, II, 30) But the larger ontological base in which Emerson's political thinking is set, involves, as we have seen, an inversion of the Platonic ontology emphasizing the replacement of a natural law or teleology with making.

Emerson's revision of Plato can be read in Plato's own writing where the (as it were) Emersonian position is a major countertheme. The large generalization about Plato made by Emerson, noted previously, that Plato embraced "both sides of every great question," while untrue of Plato, is true about Emerson. This two-sidedness is perceived by Emersonians as his "dialectic," as his balancing of "imaginative autonomy as against Necessity, ...transparency as against enforced opaqueness."[16] This balancing or the seeming contradictory embrace of opposites is evident throughout Emerson's thinking. Thus, the I is not I; freedom, though it is whim, is also fatal; and, most important of all, the one is many and the many is one. "The Same, the Same," Emerson declared; distinctions are ignorance. ("P", W, IV, 49) Emerson's doctrine of unity or of the one and many is the prototype of his thinking. This is a fact of great importance, but not only because the "problem of the one and the many," to cite Friedlander's typically incisive summary of the matter, "is the fundamental problem of philosophical reasoning."[17]

The problem of the one and the many, therefore of language, is the problem of civilization or of cosmology. How men perceive the one and the many affects the order of human history hence also its course. Emerson's aspiration to excel in divinity or to create things with words means that he would replace reality as given with his words or concepts so that these shall become real: words shall become action. As a theoretical matter this places man in the condition of Cratylus as described in Plato and Aristotle. This is the position of denying the law of noncontradiction and of being compelled, as a result, to forego all language, relying instead upon simply moving one's finger. Cratylus' purpose, like Emerson's, was to embrace two sides of every question, to show the truth of contradiction. But this truth is founded solely upon the existential preeminence of language, not on the world to which language refers. Yet we know that language is for Emerson the "other half" of man. In other words, Emerson substitutes the realm "of the one and the many that belong[s] to the world of becoming and passing away [i.e., the apeiron, for]...conceptual or ideal unity, *oneness*."[18] The unity and imperishability of language is the apeirontic deception to which Emerson succumbed. Friedlander writes: "It is characteristic of the *logoi* (of thought, of speech, of sentences) that they combine the one and the many. Here the combination is obvious because the possibility of any responsible speech is based on it." But, Friedlander continues, the "very significance" of language in the apprehension of the whole "entails the danger of eristic abuse."[19] The danger is that language, because it combines the one and the many as the condition for responsible speech, will be mistaken for the one and the many simply.

This is a very important point and justifies a digression of several paragraphs. And, because common sense recoils upon hearing that Emerson or anyone suggests that snakes and madhouses can be replaced with "your own world" – what Emerson cries out for at the conclusion of *Nature* – we are disposed to dismiss such ideas, regarding them either as foolish or as high idealism, and at all events of no importance to practical life, to social and political affairs. But this is a mistake. Poets, especially Emersonian ones, are devoted to practical affairs. We may easily see why by answering the question: What is the cultural effect of "eristic abuse" of language? The effect is this: the "open society." We mean by this political phrase the social principle of radical toleration. These political and social terms describe the ethos of social science, the formal and implicit ideas of which saturate contemporary life. According to social science, all "value judgments" count as equal or "relative" on the ground that truths about values are inaccessible. We may also call relativism gnostic because the practical result of the ideal that values are equal is to qualify all speakers, regardless of their wisdom or their study of the facts, as final judges, as antiphilosophers, but in the same sense that they are completed philosophers or those whose quest for wisdom is over. Since there can be no appeal from an individual's judgment to truth, except to the truth that every individual's opinion is as good, i.e., as true, as anyone else's, each man may be said to possess the power of the divine, i.e., the knowledge of good and evil.

Only the gnostic seeks to enshrine his word in place of reality regardless of what other men know or have known. Modern movements for peace and liberation are gnostic in this sense because they contemptuously disregard the history and experience of mankind, calling it "realism." In place of reality they demand an ideal, some future condition that begins with them. This ideal shall alter men and reality by the dogmatism which brought such movements into being in the first place. This lust for certitude, dressed outwardly in the habiliments of toleration and indeterminacy, is Emerson's stock in trade. It has become, a century after his death, the common coin of popular speech. Emerson's relevance to social and political life could hardly be greater. In sum, the real meaning of radical toleration – that is, of eristic abuse – is absolute intolerance on all levels and on the highest level; the philosophic eristic abuse is a priori dogmatism or the prohibition of philosophy. Finally, where each individual establishes his own final truths it follows that justice is equivalent to preventing any imposition of one person's opinion upon others. In this formula we recognize the prototype of ethical and legal discourse in our time. In particular, this formula informs our discussions about speech. The idea that speech is free because truth is relative is a commonplace of popular understanding.

But the relativism of speech can only mean that speech and gesture, i.e., action, are identical. Here is the theoretical point we hoped to reach. This point, now popularly accessible to us in such sensational legal rulings extending the idea of speech to nude public dancing, is the one that reduced the pre-Socratic relativist Cratylus to regarding the movement of his finger as the only permissible speech. It was, in fact, relativists such as Heraclitus of the ancient world who, considering everything flux and incertitude, insisted, as Emerson later did (and with infinitely greater aspirations) that contradictory statements are simultaneously true, i.e., that "value judgments" are equal. Speakers who say that truths do not exist, to be logical, must assume the silence of Cratylus or else contradictorily regard all speech as gesture, including, naturally, the proposition that truths do not exist. It is highly relevant that Aristotle's attack on the ideas of Heraclitus as attempting to evade the principle of noncontradiction (holding that contradictory statements cannot simultaneously be true) is the *locus classicus* of all attacks upon relativism. It was Aristotle who also defined man as the being who speaks intelligently about good and evil, i.e., about "values." Man Thinking is precisely he who, contrary to Aristotle as well as to the traditions stemming from him and from Plato, speaks "hard words" about what he thinks is true today, and then does the same hard speaking tomorrow, "though it contradict every thing" said the day before. ("SR", CW, II, 33) For Emerson's Man Thinking "good and bad are but names readily transferable to that or this; the only right is what is after my constitution, the only wrong what is against it." (Ibid., 30) Let us return to our discussion of Plato to consider his treatment of Emerson's doctrine in its most critical form, namely regarding freedom or the self.

Plato responds to the Emersonian doctrine of the one and the many, according to which the self is not "'thou; nor are others, others; nor am I,I,'" in the *Philebus*, in the following exchange with Protarchus. ("P", W, IV, 50, quoting "Krishna")

[R]eally it is a remarkable thing to say that many are one, and one is many; a person who suggests either of these things may well encounter opposition.

Protarchus: Do you mean a person who says that I, Protarchus, though I am one human being am nevertheless many Protarchuses of opposite kinds...though I am really always the same person?

Socrates: That isn't what I mean....Almost everyone agrees nowadays that there is no need to concern oneself with things like that, feeling that they are childish, obvious, and a great nuisance to argument.[20]

But Emerson's I, who is *other*, is the model of freedom. Emerson teaches that freedom is the Good or the highest good; that it is virtue. Emerson's is a freedom from the impingements of the social as such, and from the self as well, so that Man Thinking may draw a new circle absolutely his own. In the expression of this freedom, an imitation of God, or the circle on a sphere, man is all and man is one. More, freedom or *whim* is also necessity or not choosing: the self, liberated by desire from choice, is liberated from "all mean egotism." This we shall see later was the final goal and final paradox of Emerson's teaching. It is the resolution of all Emerson's paradoxes.

By naming freedom as the highest virtue, Emerson's claim of independence is made not alone or even primarily against society. His claim of freedom is made against reality itself and against the cosmos: Man Thinking makes his own world. No more complete rejection of the Platonic is conceivable. Free of reality, thus free to create his own world, the real world vanishes. Emerson's freedom includes freedom from nature. Freedom is expressed by Man Thinking's "doctrine ever new and sublime; that there is One Man." ("AS", CW, I, 53) The soul, we already know, is one, i.e., the self, which "simply is." It is beyond good and evil, beyond nature. Freedom is the Good and the Good is the One or Man Thinking. Man Thinking, as the cosmion or what is, makes the study of self, not the study of reality, the most important subject. But if Man Thinking is the One, thus the Good, what becomes of the self, of individuality and contingency, of choices?

Emerson solves the problem of the Good, of freedom or Man Thinking, by identifying the one and the many of speech as the real. He substitutes the divinity of eloquence for the divinity of the cosmos. Plato has been turned on his head. Emerson's One is the apeiron hypostatized. The One is the product of human making, or language. This making is a timeless undertaking. Here then is the source of Emerson's animus against history and memory. Timelessness is the condition for the overcoming of the apeiron (necessarily, since the apeiron is that mode of being bounded by time). Creation is necessarily the overcoming of the apeiron. This is exactly the thing Emerson intends that Man Thinking should do when he puts nature under foot. Freedom is endless experimentation or change. Change or making and creativity is not required to pay the penalty of time. Change and experimentation have the power of the One. Man is free, or One, so long as he creates. Free from evil and free from time, Man is immortal thus he is the Good. Of course, there is no history. Creativity also requires that nothing outside of man's making shall be different from what man says it is. But this application of the principle of the one and the many within the system of language-making, to which the one and the many is essential as the means of coherence, is an eristic deception: it cuts off apprehension of the ground by establishing as it also proscribes all attempts to call language to account by referring to reality. Such an accounting is a limitation upon making or human creativity. As a practical matter, Emerson's Platonism, as we have seen, is a swarm of contradictions and paradoxes. Considered as an ethical system, Emerson's ideas issue in tolerance and benevolence. But here contradiction becomes intolerable in the telltale identification of the good, of freedom, and the pleasurable. Thus change and endless experimentation are not really one but apeirontic, a "motley," as Plato says.[21] Apeirontic freedom is necessarily many. This sort of freedom, as one astute observer has said, calls for the "reduction of history to an illusion and of experience to a pin-point present."[22] These pin-points are Emerson's circles: the "many" that are also One.

In the *Philebus*, the subject of the one and many is introduced following a discussion of pleasure. The connection, Friedlander remarks, "seems arbitrary in the sense that we might have come upon [the question of the one and the many from the discussion, say, of shapes, as of pleasure.] Yet, for this very reason, the connection is not accidental, for the problem of the one and the many is the fundamental problem of philosophical reasoning itself."[23] But there is, we suggest, yet another reason why Plato introduces the subject of the one and the many with a discussion of pleasure. He wishes to show, in explaining why pleasure qua pleasure is not a unity – namely, because it is a "motley" – that the confusion of the many with the one is "nonsense." Just as we would not call all shapes one or equal because every shape is a shape, round shapes as well as square ones, so not all pleasure is one. The pleasurable cannot be the Good because it is not One but many. The pleasurable is apeirontic or things; it perishes. Recall that the identification of pleasure with the good was the basis of Kren's and Rappoport's indictment of Judaism in Chapter 2.

To summarize then, Emerson inverts the Platonic relationships of being and substitutes eristic for dialectic by means of the poet's man-creating words. The product of these words is unified humanity. In keeping with his vision, Emersonian explanation describes a circle. Emerson labors to make "a new circle" literally reflecting his dominating aspiration to render words into things, thought into making, or action. Thus, poetry is the begetting of "Messias." (JMN, XIII, 259) But this wish of Emerson's to draw a new circle casts him in the role of the Serpent in the Garden in quite a literal way as we shall note subsequently. His wish to lose his "sempiternal memory," that he may have no knowledge but the complete knowledge that he makes himself, is the work of the poet's eye which "can integrate all the parts." (*N*, CW, I, 9) The poet's eye is the transparent eyeball, nature being "put... forth through us." (Ibid., 38)

The perfect circle drawn by each Man Thinking, although it is a creation and not therefore artificial or whimsical – his own world – is necessary, even so. Again, the Good is plainly not One. Emerson writes in "Circles": "no evil is pure,...hell itself...[is not] without its extreme satisfactions." ("C", CW, II, 188)[24] And if the Good is not

One it is because it is many. Although Bloom discovers Emerson's anticipation of "moralists" such as Yvor Winters to be ripe with an "astonishingly formidable irony," in fact, Emerson's self-defense of his "circularity" is very nearly a caricature of the romantic free spirit.[25] Consider if Emerson's comments upon justice summon up a vision of a Grecian philosopher or of Harold Skimpole, Dickens' feckless idealist of *Bleak House*.

> One man's justice is another's injustice; one man's beauty, another's ugliness; one man's wisdom, another's folly....One man thinks justice consists in paying debts....But...which debt must I pay first, the debt to the rich...the debt of money, or the debt of thought to mankind, of genius to nature? For you, O broker, there is no other principle but arithmetic. For me, commerce is of trivial import. (Ibid., 187)

Freedom is here liberation with no object except itself. "Man is all," and nature vanishes. Naturally, everything is every other thing. Man the one is "experimenter."

> Lest I should mislead any when I have my own head, and obey my whims, let me remind the reader that I am only an experimenter. Do not set the least value on what I do, or the least discredit on what I do not, as if I pretended to settle anything as true or false. I unsettle all things. No facts are to me sacred; none are profane; I simply experiment, an endless seeker, with no Past at my back. (Ibid., 188)

If nature is a man's double and he its creator, if too the past has vanished together with swine and madhouses, transforming memory into a dream of God, will not freedom as absolute whim be identical to the most complete necessity, to not choosing at all? If freedom is to become spontaneous willing without mediation, is it not also, godlike or Nietzsche-like, without choices? We must explore Emerson's quarrel with "books" and the past to see how he invited these consequences. He invited the consequences of divinity by way of the "perfect circle." ("SR", CW, II,42)

Notes

1. Ralph L. Rusk, *The Life of Ralph Waldo Emerson* (New York, 1949), 94.

2. Emerson Sermon 134 quoted in R.A. Yoder, *Emerson and the Orphic Poet in America* (Berkeley, 1978), 10.

3. See F. DeWolfe Miller, *Christopher Pearse Cranch and his Caricature of New England Transcendentalism* (Cambridge, Massachusetts, 1951). A discussion of Cranch's drawings follows below.

4. Leo Strauss, "What is Political Philosophy?" in *What is Political Philosophy?* (Glencoe, Illinois, 1959), 39.

5. Harold Bloom, *Figures of Capable Imagination* (New York, 1976), 49.

6. John Q. Anderson, *The Liberating Gods; Emerson on Poets and Poetry* (Coral Gables, Florida, 1971), 57.

7. "SR", "C", CW, II, 33, 190. Emerson's wish to "lose" his "sempiternal memory and to do something without knowing how or why" is the condition for having "no Past at [his]...back" (ibid., 188). The term sempiternal qualifies eternity as having a beginning but no end. A new circle means then an "eternity" that begins with me, the new circle-maker.

8. Harold Bloom, Review of Quentin Anderson, *The Imperial Self* in *Commentary*, 52 (1971), 88.

9. Noam Chomsky, *Problems of Knowledge and Freedom* (New York, 1971), 50, Chomsky's political views, especially regarding Judaism, are akin to Emerson's. The relationship deserves study beyond the interesting analysis of Sampson who quite correctly regards Chomsky as a "typical socialist" for whom the idea of creativity (and freedom) "turns out to mean what many of us would call 'uncreative.'" Geoffrey Sampson, *Liberty and Language* (Oxford, 1979), 210.

10. Miller, *Christopher Pearse Cranch*, 33. Cranch's drawings, mentioned here, are found in this volume.

11. Plato, *Symposium*, 189b5.

12. Ibid., 189d9–e4.

13. Ibid., 190a7–9.

14. Compare Paul Friedlander, *Plato* (3 vols.; Princeton, 1969), III, 26.

15. A. Robert Caponigri, "Brownson and Emerson; Nature and History," *New England Quarterly*, XVIII (1945), 375.

16. Bloom, *Figures of Capable Imagination*, 63.

17. Friedlander, *Plato*, III, 318.

18. Ibid.

19. Ibid., 319.

20. Plato, *Philebus*, 14c9–d9.

21. See Friedlander, *Plato*, III, 316.

22. Caponigri, "Brownson and Emerson," 371.

23. Friedlander, *Plato*, III, 318.

24. This observation shall evidently make me more sour than "even the sourest critic" according to one recent Emersonian study. See B.L. Packer, *Emerson's Fall, A New Interpretation of the Major Essays* (New York, 1982), 15. The question, and problem, of the near worshipping of Emerson by academics (and the corresponding anathematizing of dissenters) is a subject in itself. We note here that Packer, participating in these traditions, also continues the astonishingly virulent and in truth uncivil excoriation of Yvor Winters, one of two dissenters from the Emersonian consensus. Something of the tone and grace of this attack is conveyed in Packer's comment that Winters was either "careless or willfully stupid."

CHAPTER 5

Emerson and the Jews' God

Emerson's project of creativity or freedom is rooted in word-making. But words are not real. They are not live in any but a poetic sense. The success of Emerson's project, like Terach's or Nebuchadnezzar's, would empower what is not live to rule what is. The freedom Emerson craves, or divinity by means of eloquence, places him in conflict with the Second Commandment and therefore with the First as well.

The poet's inversion of Platonic symbols that we have discussed in the last chapter permits Emerson to identify Man as One. But there is no existential unity except the inverted or false one, embraced by Emerson, of the apeirontic conceived as the One; the One that is man, or universal and homogeneous man.

Emerson's unified humanity is the creation of the poet's man-creating words. The poet, for his part, is himself one with all men whose thoughts he utters, and who, for their part, recognize in the poet their deepest sense of selfhood. The source of this symmetry and unity is "nature." Emerson's explanation of nature, as we have seen, is serpentine. Even though Emerson seems to be a nature-lover, an admirer of sunsets, he is not willing to extol given beauty. Nature is the ass upon which the savior, the poet, rides. (*N*, CW, I, 25) Nature is malleable. The source of Emerson's vision, of nature and of all things, is the circle. In keeping with this vision,

Emersonian explanations articulate circles at all levels. He strives, he says, to make "a new circle." This shape reflects his preoccupation with words which he regards as things. Poetry is for Emerson the light. The poet is the eye that sees the light. The transparent eyeball is light and also seeing. Light streams into the eye and into the heart of the child. This is because poetry is language in its infancy. Like the child, primitive language is closer to nature where it expresses, like the comparison itself, the "radical correspondence between visible things and human thoughts." (N, CW, I, 19) "Infancy is the perpetual Messiah," says Emerson, just as poetry is the begetting of messiahs. (Ibid., 42; JMN, XIII, 259) This knowledge we recall is the result of the poet's eye which "can integrate all the parts." (N, CW, I, 9) The poet's eye is the transparent eyeball; nature being "put...forth through us." (Ibid., 38)

The poet turns to nature as the resource "to live," that is, he turns to nature to uncover "the sacred germ of his instinct, screened from influence." ("AS", CW, I, 61) Instinct bodies forth as "unhandselled savage nature" or pure poetry, pure undivided self, reverencing all things alike. (Ibid.) This pure being is undivided man, Emerson's Man Thinking. The unity of Man Thinking, born of "reading God directly," that is, of the unfolding of instinct ("nature") screened from influence, whether of books ("other men's transcripts of their readings") or of society (ossified readings), is the expression of self; specifically this is self-reliance. (Ibid., 57) But self is that condition of oneness that comes upon the undivided being as a consequence of his instinct. This is the liberation from all manner of dividedness, freedom from society and from other men's readings of God. Emerson describes this freedom as the "one thing which we seek with insatiable desire..., [namely] to forget ourselves, to be surprised out of our propriety, to lose our sempiternal memory, and to do something without knowing how or why; in short, to draw a new circle." ("C", CW, II, 190)

The circle, the Pythagorean symbol borrowed by the medieval church where it was a sign of heaven, had become the image of the most radical ontological equality in the minds of French and German romantics and revolutionaries by the late 18th century. In addition to the circle's connections with equality and timelessness – i.e., with ideas of equidistance, of brotherhood and the harmony of all points – the circle conveys other meanings. The circle is an ancient symbol of the sacred as human (of man as god) in which no distinction is recognized between the human and the divine. The civilizations of the Aztecs and of the preChristian Mediterranean are examples. Significantly, language in civilizations of this type plays no part in denoting the sacred since the objects of worship are inseparable from deeds and from phenomenal objects as they were to become for Man Thinking.

The poet who turns to live with "unhandselled savage nature" actually turns to live with the mind of God. "There is one mind common to all individual men. Every man is an inlet to the same and to all of the same." ("H", CW, II, 3) The poet, Man Thinking or one who is undivided, has full access to the mind of the creator. This proposition is another way of expressing the one that precedes it. Man Thinking is in "alliance with truth and God." (*N*, CW, I, 20) Thus plainly does the poet hold the "keys of power." (Ibid., 21) The poet's access to God on the one hand, and his power to create truth by use of nature – said to be "thoroughly mediate" – on the other hand, makes the poet nothing less than the savior or son. (Ibid., 25) Nature as we have seen wears the aspect of Jesus; it is in truth the ass upon which the savior rides.

As mediator, nature echoes the Ten Commandments or indeed any other laws Man Thinking discovers there. Nature, says Emerson, "does not exist to any one or to any number of particular ends, but to numberless and endless benefit." ("MN", CW, I, 126–7) Who then can doubt, he asks, "that poetry will revive and lead in a new age?" Who can doubt, he asks yet further, here strongly hinting, as he does occasionally of his millennial purposes, that poetry "shall one day be the pole-star for a thousand years?" ("AS", CW, I, 52) Emerson's is that "new perception" that sees the whole, nature and man, as a unity, immanent and coherent. ("SR", CW, II, 39) "[A]ll organizations are radically alike." (*N*, CW, I, 26) "When we have new perception, we shall gladly disburden the memory of its hoarded treasures as old rubbish." ("SR", CW, II, 39) These hoarded treasures, the remembrance of events of specific times, are the limitations on Man Thinking Emerson seeks to cast off. "When we have broken our god of tradition, and ceased from our god of rhetoric, then may God fire the heart with his presence." ("O-S", CW, II, 173) How completely opposite this is from the Jewish way we will shortly observe.

As nature is a metaphor of the mind, the mind being Nature or Spirit of which man is a part in his undivided state, it must follow that "[e]very universal truth which we express in words, implies or supposes every other truth." (N, CW, I, 28) The poet is creator in the finite, but his words are "messiahs," they create men: "man is the word made flesh." ("SR", CW, II, 43) The word-maker or poet bears the same relation to God that Jesus bears to God in Christian thinking or that Torah bears to God in Judaism. By God, however, Emerson means the poet or savior, the undivided self who makes men into flesh with words. God in the infinite or the One, is that unity of mind with itself, or freedom; God is the "great circle on a sphere, comprising all possible circles." (N, CW, I, 28) And how many circles are there? As many as there are new circle makers, i.e., poets, or those who "seek with insatiable desire...to be surprised out of...[their] propriety...to draw a new circle." ("C", CW, II, 190) The truth is one and many: the "endless benefit" of nature is matched by endless truth. "Every such truth is the absolute Ens seen from one side. But it has innumerable sides." (N, CW, I, 28) Regarding this image, in which Emerson reverses the relationship of the thing that exists and the ground of its existence so that he at his will becomes the ground of things, Marion Montgomery has made the following observation. "Here," says Montgomery, "one has a modern gnostic use of St. Thomas's ens....The thing is absolute, but it owes its absolute being to the mind that wills it." And, of almost equal importance, Montgomery also understands, this "seemingly benevolent Emerson...[though he] invokes a term like God or Universal Spirit: the only divinity Emerson ever really acknowledges is his own intellect." Emerson has his own "perfect circle."[1]

The savior is he who will bring about the "influx of spirit," inaugurating the transformation of existence, the vanishing of swine and madhouses. And this will come about when all men are equally poets, i.e., when all men are one, thus no longer in the divided condition. This is the magical center and circle of Emerson's ontology and the seed of all his paradoxes – when one man, Emerson (i.e., Man as One), is poet, then one man is God. What is this absolute truth universally found in every other truth? Certainly it is creation. Creation is what springs up in man once the dead weight of influence is lifted from him. "The soul active sees absolute truth; and utters truth, or creates." ("AS", CW, I, 56) Creations are truth, but creations of what? Again obviously, of "my own world." Moreover, the "convertibility of every thing into every other thing," of the unity of man and nature, thus their radical alikeness (i.e., the oneness of all organization) makes the discovery of undivided self the discovery of godhood. Emerson's unity is then a correspondence of organizations. How are the dead weights of influence to be lifted from man? What are these weights? Emerson answers these questions as one; the dead weights of influence are those of "nature" and "books."

The correct perception of nature is the first step toward discovery of the self and this discovery is the unburdening of dead weights. The discovery of freedom or creation is the next and final step: the creation of nature and the banishment of swine and madhouses. "As the world was plastic and fluid in the hands of God, so it is ever to so much of his attributes as we bring to it." ("AS", CW, I, 64) Truth, in sum, is the equivalent of self-reliance. "It is like a great circle on a sphere, comprising all possible circles." (N, CW, I, 28) This condition, all limits passed, is what Emerson names freedom. His transcendentalism and his idealism are a transcending of all facts by means of apeirontic investment of every fact, of all fact as such, and not the transcending of any discrete fact within the apeiron. We have touched on Emerson's proposals for Man Thinking's liberation from nature by putting nature under foot. His doctrine of books is an intimate part of man's release from the confinements of nature. And just as Emerson introduces us to the delights of conquering nature by way of a seemingly benevolent concern for the nature of common sense, so he invites us to consider the irrelevance of books by praising them and scholarship generally as among the highest and best things.

Emerson begins by crediting "the mind of the Past" as the second greatest influence, next to nature, in forming the self-consciousness of Man Thinking. ("AS", CW, I, 55) But as nature's work is in yielding to "the dominion of man," history as the accumulation of poetic utterances is the servant of the present. Man Thinking, who craves to read "God directly," has no time to waste in reading books. They are "other men's transcripts of their readings." (Ibid., 57) For although books "are the best of things, well used," they are for use only during "the scholar's idle times." (Ibid., 56, 57) The process of bookish influence, "the best type of the influence of the past," is not progressive, but upward and altogether personal. (Ibid., 55) Emerson describes the process this way: the "scholar of the first age received into him the world around; brooded thereon; gave it the new arrangement of his own mind, and uttered it again." (Ibid.) As for the value of this utterance "it depends on how far [it carried] the process...of transmuting life into truth." (Ibid.) The "purity and imperishableness of the product," preserved in a book, is never "quite perfect....[No] artist entirely exclude[s] the conventional, the local, the perishable from his book." (Ibid.) For this reason the first age and all succeeding ages are never sufficient for the purposes of the present. "Each age...must write its own books; or rather, each generation for the next succeeding. The books of an older period will not fit this." (Ibid., 56) What Emerson gives with one hand – respect for the past, for books, he takes with the other hand – creation, so that he may "sing a song of himself." Clearly truth has no meaning but making or creation. It involves an overcoming of past creation not any building upon it. "Genius," says Emerson with perfect consistency, "always looks forward." (Ibid., 57) It can look nowhere else. "All history becomes subjective; in other words, there is properly no History....Every mind must know the whole lesson for itself – must go over the whole ground. What it does not see, what it does not live, it will not know." ("H", CW, II, 6) In this way time's injustices are rectified; the experimenter has now no past at his back. "Give me insight into to-day," Emerson said, "and you may have the antique and future worlds." ("AS", CW, I, 67) Here then is the pin-point present, actually the eternal present. This is the fixed point or unity.

Unity is Emerson's great object. What is unity and how is it achieved? This is the freedom to which all of Emerson's philosophy aspires. Unity is what Emerson seeks as man and poet. Moreover, this "new and sublime doctrine" has been discovered by means of poetry and is achievable by it. The poet can bring about the transformation of man the farmer, man the shopkeeper, man the teacher, into man the One. The poet's eye, combining the power to see and the means to create, is transformed as it transforms. The poet is the eye of man who, because he is One, can have no other I. By means of word-making the poet "begets Messias." For words are not things only, and possessed of the capacity to "bleed." Words are "initiative, spermatic, prophesying[,] man-making." (JMN, VIII, 148) Recall that when the poet speaks, his comments are "ejaculated as Logos or Word." The carnal, indeed the onanistic, language faithfully portrays Emerson's eros.

The Emersonian project is then not merely antihistorical as Caponigri has said. It is also not enough to say that Emerson's intention is antiphilosophical. Emerson's goal is certainly what Bloom claims it is – divinity. If, as Bloom says, what the poet enters upon "when he begins his life cycle as a poet, is in every sense a process of divination," or competition with god, it is fitting to ask what god Emerson competed with. The answer to this question cannot be doubted. Emerson sought to enthrone the god who is "One Man" in place of the God who is One; in place of the God of the Jews.

Having begun our study with a consideration of Yehuda Bauer's observation that Jewhatred is a phenomenon that persists in time with changes of language only, that Jewhatred is in fact a historical manifestation of idol worship, we are now in a position to suggest what this means as a philosophic proposition. The persistence of Jewhatred is a unity of a kind within the apeirontic field. It is as it were a counter to the theme of One or Unity, the actual counter to the apeiron. This subject, certainly among the most fascinating, is, as we saw in the opening chapter, among the least explored of all secular themes in Western historiography where it is relegated to the harmless, and altogether reversed position of an instance of "intolerance," thus an enemy of progressive forces. This liberal understanding of Jewhatred as equivalent to any hated thing or idea is itself an expression of Jewhatred in that it universalizes or de-Judaizes Judaism.

"The Hebrew religion," wrote Vico in *The New Science*, "was founded by the true God on the prohibition of the divination on which all the gentile nations arose." This axiom, he explained, "is one of the principle reasons for the division of the entire world of the ancient nations into Hebrews and gentiles."[2] The prohibition of divination to which Vico refers is that of the Second Commandment against "idolatry." This prohibition is also the first of the Noahide commandments binding on non-Jews.

Concerning the Second Commandment, Cynthia Ozick's comment, already quoted, that it "runs against the grain of our social nature, indeed against human imagination" is pertinent. The Second Commandment or "monotheism," is what Emerson called the "terrific Jewish Idea before which ages were driven like sifted snow, which all the literatures of the world...tingle with." (JMN, VII, 321) Emerson sought to liberate himself from the terrific Jewish Idea. "[W]e sleek dapper men," he said, "have quite got free of that old reverence, have heard new facts on metaphysics, & are not quite ready to join any new church." (Ibid.) The Second Commandment expresses the same prohibition, elaborated in Plato, against hypostatization of elements within the apeiron, or against the flooding of consciousness with the Beyond. Both movements entail the destruction of the metaxy, the structural equivalent of which in Judaism is the oral and written Torah. The "terrific Jewish Idea" or monotheism is also Plato's One.

Ozick's comment, describing a constant temptation to exodus from the conditions of existence in the metaxy, may be applied to Emerson as to the "ancient nations." But Emerson's project is entirely modern in its self-understanding of Judaism as archaic and exclusive; as enslavement to books, the past, consistency. These are the obstacles in the way of Man Thinking. Liberation from them is Emerson's conscious and ultimate purpose. Accordingly Emerson aims his revisionary effort at the heart of Judaism; at God and the Second Commandment. "You cannot say God, blood, & hell too little," we remember him saying. "Always suppose God. The Jew named him not." (JMN, IX, 273)

Emerson disdained the role of heroic crusader, preferring that of liberating god instead. Thus Emerson went beyond the aspirations of either the Hellenes or the Church. Unlike those ancient foes of Judaism, Emerson hoped to bring about the supersession of God, in addition to that of Torah and Israel. The Church, although it considered the land of Israel superseded by Jesus, its holiness proportional to its non-Jewish character, nevertheless looked upon the Torah as prefatory, and upon God as the father. The Jews themselves remained a negative witness. But Emerson's revision of Judaism is radical and thorough. It begins with revision of God. Naturally the Church, and all that comes after it, and not just Torah and Israel, are superseded. And the poet himself, "incurring the disdain of the able...[;] loss and scorn," becomes the new suffering servant. ("AS", CW, I, 62) As for the persecution of the Jew, it is perhaps a thing almost fitting when considered in light of Milton's comment that "'the Jews thought it too much license to follow the charming pipe of him who sounded and proclaimed liberty and relief to all distresses.'" (JMN, IV, 282)

The charming piper Emerson had in mind proclaimed liberty of a certain kind. The description of liberty is naturally Emerson's continuing concern. Because Emerson considered liberty to be making or creation he spoke of liberty as a love of "change" or "experimentalism." Scholarly practice, for reasons elaborated earlier, has been to accord the honorific name democracy to a love of liberty as change and experiment. But this is not theoretically sound; democracy is a political term not an ontological one. The effect of his substitution is to protect a philosophical position made to do the work of philosophical questioning. Moreover the name democracy obscures the theoretical base of Emerson's thinking about liberty. It obscures the character of the charming piper.

Emerson's love to "unsettle," his insistent incantation that everything is false, expresses a certain gnostic orthodoxy, or Orphism. Bloom writes: "Doom, for the Orphic, was to fall victim to repetition compulsion, and so to carry water in a sieve in Hades. Every hateful exclusiveness ever felt by a Western poet [and, Bloom notes elsewhere, any "sensitive American"] is ultimately Orphic."[3] Emerson's revision of the "absolutism" that is Judaism emerges in his Orphic doxology in *Nature*. The faith of the fathers, symbolic of all hateful mediation between God and the spirit imagined to be imprisoned in the world, is exactly the faith of the Jews.

Emerson's most important, and his most shocking conception is his revision of the "terrific Jewish Idea." Emerson was constrained to invent a speaker, the Orphic poet of *Nature*, to deliver this idea in its first and starkest form. That Emerson, the poet who sought to make the real symbolic of poetry, should seek out disguises and shun frankness is genuinely ironic. But language is not competent to stand in place of reality. All the more difficult is it when the "reality" in question, Emerson's thought, roots in the reality he seeks to supplant with eloquence.

Emerson's theme of freedom or self-reliance, embodied in his revision of Judaism about to be detailed here, was not openly avowed. Before turning to consider the Orphic poet's comments on Judaism it will be useful to attend to Emerson's more visible, outward meanings. Although Emerson did not ultimately mean by *freedom* the things mid-19th century Americans meant by freedom or self-reliance, his exoteric meanings are nevertheless familiar and acceptable ones. Self-reliance, symbolic of Emerson's "undivided" man or unity, bears only a semantic kinship to such subjects as "civil rights" or equal protection under the law or rather these and other usages are disguises for less welcome or opposite ideas. Civil rights, for example, are at length unintelligible in context of Emersonian self-reliance. But Emerson rang the changes on the word freedom to smooth the way for a reception of his ultimate meanings. His readers and listeners could scarcely have supposed their daring dissenter's embrace of the Higher Criticism or of freedom as a release from "convention" would involve them in the raw consequences of his attacks upon exclusivity. These ramifications involved not only the elimination of property (thus the end of political freedom). They also involved the unseating of God as making way for a new freedom; the liberation from all "mean egotism," that is, the liberation from choice.

Emerson suggests his purpose from within the protecting shell of contemporary dissenting religion. He is openly critical of Christianity. In particular Emerson is critical of the then reigning extremity of unorthodox but still respectable Christianity or Unitarianism. Eminently vulnerable, Unitarian doctrine proposed a natural and scientific witness to the Bible's miracles, thus forcing its defenders into the impossible position of showing how these miracles could withstand the "devastating analysis," as two latter-day debunkers of "miracles" have put it, of the German higher critics.[4]

Nineteenth-century Unitarianism was as its name implies a Christianity gone nearly beyond the touchstones of Christianity. The divinity of Jesus is worn thin in Unitarianism. Having gone this far it was not easy to defend the religious aspects of Unitarianism without a seeming compromise with its own critique of the trinity. Charges of hypocrisy against the Unitarian faithful and embarrassed protestations by the now "conservative" defenders of Unitarianism typified the predictable and unedifying contests of Unitarians and Transcendentalists familiar to all students of this period. The debate was in fact not substantially different from that in our own day between liberal egalitarians and so-called radicals or communists. But Emerson's criticisms of Unitarianism and of Christianity were free of the heroic ponderosities of writers such as Theodore Parker. Emerson was much clearer than Parker or Alcott about what the proper object of religious criticism should be. This object, the Jews' God, Emerson approaches with circumspection.

No generations have been without their benevolent men who condemned hatred of the Jews. But condemnation of this type is invariably a condemnation of the reasons for an earlier hatred, this being, as we noted in another context, nothing but the change of language that guides and disguises the persistence of Jewhatred. For example, medieval Jewhatred proceeds to antisemitism, and antisemitism to anti-Zionism, each new Jewhating form finding justification in high-sounding denunciations of previous forms. The hatred, that is, continues with new reasons, and the new reasons are founded in benevolence. Emerson recorded his pity for the Jews of Italy locked up "like dogs," and he also identified the Jew as usurer. (JMN, IV, 282) He traded, in other words, upon the premodern benevolence according to which Judaism was cruel, especially to Christians.

The situation of Jewhatred in the modern period typified by a rejection of all religion as "particularistic" and not "universalistic" has deepened not lessened the association of benevolence and the hatred of Judaism. It is the modern distinction between Judaism and Jews, along with the emancipation of Jews, hence the creation of antireligious Jews, that has made Jewhatred truly universal, a world-historical force and concept. This point was emphasized in Chapter 2. Modern Jewhatred, in other words, is possessed of vastly greater power as a universal ideal among men because this ideal is no other than the apeirontic opposite to the unity of God as One now raised to the level of an eschatological faith for fulfillment in this world. Of course it is the French Revolutionary ideal with regard to the Jews that is the archetype of the distinction between universalism and particularism. Jews, that is, were to be accepted as men but not as Jews. In other words, the French Revolution looks toward the liberation of man, of society, from Judaism as the basis of all human liberation.

Marx's doctrine, paraphrased here, is the quintessential expression of modern benevolence as Jewhatred, not less but most of all because it is enunciated by a Jew, the grandson of a rabbi, who willingly and eagerly renounces Judaism as a conversion not only of himself but of all mankind.[5] The hatred of Jews here becomes reactionary and particularistic. It becomes, like Judaism itself, unpeaceable and intolerant of difference and therein malevolent. We may say that the language of Jewhatred has changed, as Bauer contends, but with a new and far greater ambiguity than ordinary language or at least popular language can tolerate. The Jew himself, so far as he is a modern man, has been implicated in the ideals of benevolence. The remark of Ellen Emerson, the poet's daughter quoted earlier, takes on new meaning in view of these points.

Ellen, it will be remembered, had registered her incredulity at the poetess Emma Lazarus who had in Ellen's opinion so naively and ingenuously admitted to being a Jewess. More, she admitted to belief in Judaism. Emerson and his audiences held similar ideas about Judaism. Too, the traditions of anti-Jewish expression of the type we have already noted in Emerson's correspondence were likewise unexceptionable. In sum, "antisemitism" was not remarkable in America at Emerson's time. It is important for us to know this not only to appreciate what Emerson could and did say, but to recognize what even he, and in the vocabulary of his day, dared not to say. The attitude of contemporary Americans toward Judaism was consistent with Emerson's critique. No less a figure than Thomas Jefferson, as we have already noted, pronounced Judaism distastefully antique and illiberal. He considered it particularistic.

The criticism of Judaism as particularism is the mark of modern benevolence. Judaism is here emblematic of the failure of all religion to satisfy the criteria of science and modernist reason just as it had once been emblematic of the failure of Jews to recognize the new religion of Christianity. Accordingly Judaism was now barbaric. Emerson shared with Jefferson the view that Judaism and the Jews' God were cruel, needing reformation. Christians, said Emerson, "leave the ritual, the offering, & the altar of Moses[,] we cast off the superstitions that were the swaddling clothes of Christianity." (JMN, III, 61)

Emerson had no need to justify to his audiences the view that Judaism was false, superseded by Christianity. But this presupposition about Judaism was useful to him in view of his wider purpose. He wanted to show that the Jews' God was also false and superseded. It was expedient, in other words, to broach this more sweeping and of course antiChristian idea by way of the accepted view of Judaism and Jews. Emerson's approach to Judaism as particularism is a model of its type.

Emerson attacks the Jews' God by a seeming embrace of Christianity. The Jews' Bible he attacks by means of a seeming solicitude for Jews as people. Thus Emerson advises Christians what to do if "a man claims to know and speak of God, and carries you backward to the phraseology of some old mouldered nation in another country, in another world." He advises that one should "believe him not." ("SR", CW, II, 38) But at the same time Emerson dismisses the letter of the Bible, he takes care to single out Moses as an early Man Thinking. Emerson delivers his praise of Moses in a context of disparagement for "those foolish Israelites," whose "foolishness," however, resided precisely in their following Moses to another nation, in another country, in another world.

"[T]he highest merit we ascribe to Moses, Plato, and Milton," wrote Emerson, "is that they set at naught books and traditions, and spoke not what men but what they thought." (Ibid., 27) A doubtful trio, the statement is also radically hostile to Judaism and to Moses. Certainly Moses did not claim to write what he thought, but only to record what God spoke. And Emerson's Man Thinking, who, like Moses, "[l]ong...must stammer in his speech," is cured by learning to speak what men, in their ultimate unity with all men and nature, know to be their own thoughts. ("AS", CW, I, 62) Others "drink his words because he fulfils for them their own nature; the deeper he dives into his privatest secretest presentiment,...he finds this is the most acceptable, most public, and universally true." (Ibid., 63) What Emerson means by "most true" is most creative; the desire of all men, discoverable in the undivided state, to make their own world. But Moses' stammer was cured in an opposite fashion for an opposite purpose.

Moses was cured of slow speech by speaking what men never heard before. The import of Moses' stammer derives from its association with his speaking, as distinguished from the utterances of God. We may recur here to our identification of Emerson's Platonism with the Socratic Protagoras. Is it not the Protagorean curriculum to make the worse appear the best cause, therein to confound good with evil and to destroy philosophy? This curriculum roots in the wish to substitute language for reality, man for God. Moses' speech, his language, is designed for opposite purposes. Emerson's Man Thinking vaticinates as he speaks. This is because

Man Thinking reads God directly. He is then a seer and Emerson says the "seer is a sayer." ("DSA", CW, I, 84) When the poet speaks he creates. Inconsistency, far from being a sign of intellectual weakness, is the best evidence of strength. It is creation. "Speak what you think now in hard words, and to-morrow speak what to-morrow thinks in hard words again, though it contradict every thing you said to-day." ("SR", CW, II, 33) This prescription is made possible by what was for Emerson the happy coincidence of thinking with speaking, the result of empowering the poet as creator. "The mind now thinks; now acts; and each fit reproduces the other." ("AS", CW, I, 61) Again: "I run eagerly into...[the] resounding tumult. I...take my place...to suffer and to work, taught by an instinct that so shall the dumb abyss be vocal with speech." (Ibid., 59) It is important to note the surprising affinity of Emerson's pursuit of divinity by means of eloquence with Calvinism. This affinity affects Emerson's understanding of scripture and his approach to its revision. Before proceeding with a review of the actual revisions Emerson made of biblical texts, it will be instructive to consider the Calvinist aspect of Emerson's theology.

Although Emerson's theology is of course opposite to Calvin's, Emerson representing a step beyond the furthest extreme of anti-Calvinism or Unitarianism, there is a connecting link and a series of ramifications relating Emerson and Calvin. This link is important because its substance is found in the idea of speech. Emerson was a Calvinist in his approach to the Bible. Calvin's bold and radical revision of the religious traditions of Christianity that preceded him, his assurance that a new world and a new truth began with him, was also Emerson's self-understanding. What Richard Hooker said of Calvin one may also say of Emerson. "Divine knowledge he gathered, not by hearing or reading so much, as by teaching others."[6] Consider Emerson's poet who, "conversing in earnest,...will find that always a material image, more or less luminous, arises in his mind, contemporaneous with every thought....[T]he blending of experience with the present action of the mind...is proper creation." (N, CW, I, 20–1)

This creativity, because it is the product of Man Thinking at his place "upon the bosom of God," that is, in the undivided condition free from the influence of books or society, provokes the thought of all men, or what would be the thought of all men if they were likewise reformed and liberated. These thoughts would effect creations of separate worlds. For this reason when the poet hears himself speak, he hears God; he hears creation proper, the circle on a sphere. "I hear myself speak as a stranger....In our way of talking, we say, that is mine, that is yours; but this poet knows well that it is not his, that it is as strange & beautiful to him as to you; he would fain hear the like eloquence at length." (JMN, IX, 72) Rousseau's better known declamations against mine and thine as the source of civilization, therefore of mankind's ruin, spring from the same aspiration to be a creator that we see here in Emerson. But Rousseau was theoretically prepared to prefer the eloquence of silence to language, fearing even language as a hateful exclusivity, an intrusion on freedom. It is well to point out that Emerson's opposition to property, implicit in his comment quoted here, was an unwonted antagonism, but one nonetheless necessarily entailed by his ideas. Although Emerson understood economics no better than his fiercely anticapitalist epigones, he was as much a principled (if not always a practical) opponent of private property as they.

Like Calvin, described by Hooker, Emerson gathered divine knowledge by teaching others. Reading God directly, Emerson is the speaker or writer of a scripture in a constant state of creation. This is the condition of its truth. Moses, on the contrary, does not possess or seek eloquence. God speaks for himself. Recall that nature in Emerson is scriptural and that it is put forth by God, by man as One, through Man Thinking. Nature therefore echoes the Ten Commandments and all other laws divined by Man Thinking. The higher law, the moral law as both Emerson and also Thoreau referred to the operations of "nature" or unity, is high and moral because it is freedom.

This is bound to be the case for Emerson who regards "every natural fact...[as] a symbol of some spiritual fact." (N, CW, I, 18) He says that every appearance in nature corresponds to some state of mind, and that state of mind can only be described by presenting the natural appearance as its picture. What is the "picture" of the Ten Commandments in nature? Is it a tree, is it some collection of human actions? Of course the Ten Commandments are sounds, an echo. They are speech, the poet's speech. "The world is emblematic. Parts of speech are metaphors because the whole of nature is a metaphor of the human mind." (Ibid., 21) Pronouns, verbs, gerunds stand for acts of mind. Nature echoes the Ten Commandments – or any number of commandments – because it "is not fixed but fluid." (Ibid., 44) Of course, it is plain that Man Thinking, not God, speaks the commandments that nature echoes. As Man Thinking speaks nature takes form. In this way shall the "abyss be vocal with speech." Without the poet's speech there can be no echo at all, no commandments at all. It is then less a command than a description of nature that Emerson gives us when he says that we must speak today in hard words, and tomorrow speak what tommorow thinks "in hard words again though it contradict everything you said to-day."

It is clear too why "picturesque language is at once a commanding certificate that he who employs it, is a man in alliance with truth and God." (Ibid., 20) Speaking of this sort is "proper creation." When nature echoes the Ten Commandments, instructing us to heed the "absolute truth," namely creation, it calls us to a new kind of prayer. This would be the "contemplation of the facts of life from the highest point of view," from the point of view of God. Unthinking man prays "to effect a private end." This, Emerson says, would be "meanness and theft. It supposes dualism and not unity in nature and consciousness. As soon as man is at one with God, he will not beg." He will not beg because prayer will have become "the spirit of God pronouncing his works good." ("SR", CW, II, 44) Is it any wonder then that "all thing are moral"? (N, CW, I, 25; "CM", CW, II, 60) How can it be otherwise if the Ten Commandments, if all "law" arises in nature as Emerson supposes? Naturally there "is a soul at the centre of nature, and over the will of every man, so that none of us can wrong the universe."("SL", CW, II, 81)

We are free. But what is it that we must do for this new freedom? We must yield first of all to a higher law than the Bible and secondly we must cast off "all mean egotism." The Bible contains, in addition to the Ten Commandments, other laws that are not only barbarous but the enemies of man's new freedom. The Bible acts to impede our freedom by encouraging a wrong opinion of books and of action, i.e., a wrong opinion of freedom. Emerson turns to the source of our wrong opinion of books, to the Bible, as the means to teach us how to read. In teaching us how to read Emerson teaches us how to speak, that is, how to be free. Revision of "the terrific Jewish Idea" begins with the revision of the Bible. Books, says Emerson, are the best of things well used, but their use is entirely a matter of personality and growth or whim. The value of books is not in our reading of them but in our writing of them just as the value of writing is in speaking. Books are not to be read but to be written. Old books are to be rewritten.

Emerson's revision of the Bible is a literal one. He shows in revising the biblical text that words are acts. In addition, he demonstrates how books are to be used. Moreover, word-making whether speaking or writing, is sacrosanct. This is because the "active soul...the one thing in the world of value" is the seat of all that is sacred. ("AS", CW, I, 56) "Nothing is at last sacred but the integrity of your own mind." ("SR", CW, II, 30) A mere book or more properly, its teaching, is not sacred. Those who, like the "foolish Israelites," "dare not yet hear God himself unless, he speak the phraseology of I know not what David, or Jeremiah, or Paul," also dare not write. (Ibid., 39) Assuredly they dare not speak. Instead they pursue a fanatical adherence to the Bible's every letter, word and sound. But the Bible is an old word-making. Its word is no longer flesh. It is not creation but a mouldered phraseology. In short the Bible is false.

Emerson's revision of the biblical text is a profound one and it ramifies broadly. Not only do the foolish Israelites recoil from speaking to God, and seek to prevent God speaking to them. Their dreadful timorousness forecloses all possibility they shall speak as gods. Thus are "men's...creeds a disease of the intellect. They say with those foolish Israelites, [and here Emerson revises the biblical text] 'Let not God speak to us, lest we die. Speak thou, speak any man with us, and we will obey.'" (Ibid., 45) The phrase, "speak any man" is Emerson's interpolation. The Bible records only the wish of the Israelites that Moses not just "any man" will speak to them. But these Emersonian Israelites who will *obey* "any man" are not simply craven. They resist true manhood. Emerson's point here, the same one the Orphic poet makes, is not made openly.

Emerson's misquotings are, we know, notorious. His affectation of negligence, as well as his real negligence, reflects his view of scholarship, thus of words and finally of his central purpose regarding the role of words in the matter of being simply. Emerson's carelessness is always to be taken as purposeful even when his mistakes can be traced to negligence. The misquotation of the biblical passage reproduced here was intentional. It is precisely wrong. Emerson leaves nothing out but instead adds something. More important still, his addition reverses the meaning of the original passage. This reversal of meaning is reinforced by Emerson's reversal of the sequence of the two sentences he quotes.

Emerson's rendition of the Bible underscores his wider purposes. Regarding books as such, Emerson's reversal and addition give striking clarification to the principle of creation, of Man Thinking in action. The literal revision of texts must include revision of the Book because a proper reading of books begins with the revision of the Jewish mode of reading the Bible without altering a letter of it. Emerson demonstrates his doctrine of "change" with reference to the Bible. We learn that no book "is quite perfect." ("AS", CW, I, 55) All books may be improved. Certainly Emerson does not mean to express the commonsense opinion that no book is flawless. Indeed insofar as a book is a transcript of a man's reading of God, it is a creation, and therefore it cannot be like any other book. In this sense a book is perfect. It is truth. Only the Bible, expressing an opposite view of books and of the reading of books, is false. The presumption of divinity made about the Bible usurps the divinity of other books, of Man Thinking. It is precisely the "act of creation," that is sacred to Emerson, not that which is "transferred to the record." (Ibid., 56) In truth the idea of scripture is an antagonism within the Emersonian circle.

Emerson's alteration of the lines from Exodus gives the strongest possible emphasis to his doctrine of books and therefore to freedom and unity, to the doctrines that man is man when he is free; that he is free when he creates, creativity being the making of the circle on a sphere which is, or will become God or man as One. We approach in this way his ideal of freedom as liberation from all mean egotism. In changing the meaning of the passage, thereby bringing the Bible into accord with his views regarding truth, Emerson directs his audiences into paths they are disposed to tread. "Everywhere," writes Emerson in the sentence following his misquotation, "I am hindered of meeting God in my brother, because he has shut his own temple doors, and recites fables merely of his brother's, or his brother's brother's God. Every new mind is a new classification." ("SR", CW, II, 45) The Israelites were foolish, in other words, because they did not realize they could, like "any man," speak with God or be spoken to by God without waiting for Moses to tell them what God had to say to them. But the Bible, in addition to stating that Moses, not "any man," may be spoken to by God, also does not consider the Israelites foolish, rather it considers them wise for not wanting to be spoken to by God.

Following the original verse in which the Israelites plead with Moses that they not be spoken to, Moses is instructed to listen to the divine voice which the body of the Jewish people will hear from him. "And the Lord said unto Moses, I come unto thee in a thick cloud, that the people may hear when I speak with thee, and believe you [Moses] for ever."[7] The Israelites were aware that only Moses and not they were to hear the word of God. Emerson knew of course that the Exodus passage he quoted does not condemn the Israelites as foolish, just as he also knew, as any Unitarian minister would, that the Israelites are praised later, in Deuteronomy, not blamed (as he blames them), for declining to hear God's word. Again Moses reports God's utterances:

> I have heard the voice of the words of this people, which they have spoken unto thee [to Moses] [viz., 5:27, "Go thou [Moses] near, and hear all that the Lord our God shall say; and speak thou unto us"] they have well [said] all that they have spoken.[8]

Any "foolishness" in the Israelites' behavior resides altogether in the direction opposite to Emerson's meaning, namely that they should have presumed God would speak to them. Moses acknowledges the Jews' fears that God might address them, saying, "Fear not [i.e., do not fear dying. You will not be spoken to by God] for God is come to prove you...that his fear may be before your faces."[9]

Emerson's revision has an unmistakable purpose, as shocking as it is bold. It has the effect of equating God with man, reading with speaking. Where the Bible says God will speak to Moses only, and only Moses may speak to the Israelites, Emerson's revision insinuates that any man may read God directly. Rewriting about speaking – especially God's speaking – has the character of divinity, of man speaking as God. Proposing in his revision of the biblical text that any man may speak to the Israelites, Emerson not only shows how anyone may read God directly, he demonstrates that when one reads God directly, i.e., writes the Bible, one learns to speak. Speaking is divine, as we know from the fact that Moses, in speaking to the Israelites, speaks what God directed him to speak. Once again we are witness to the piquancy of Bloom's observation that Emerson was too impatient to wait for God or even for mysticism. When Emerson speaks of being "at one with God" he utters no minister's platitude. Prayer, Emerson has instructed us, is not petition or praise of God. It is not a colloquy of any sort, such a thing is contemptible for man. Rather prayer "is the soliloquy of a beholding and jubilant soul." ("SR", CW, II, 44) The soliloquy of the Orphic poet is prayer of this sort.

Notes

1. Marion Montgomery, "Emerson and the Emptying of Nature," *Center Journal*, 1 (1981), 31–32.

2. Giambattista Vico, *The New Science* ed., Thomas Goddard Bergin and Max Fisch (Ithaca, New York, 1968), 68.

3. Harold Bloom, *The Anxiety of Influence* (New York, 1973), 15; Harold Bloom, *Figures of Capable Imagination* (New York, 1976), 54.

4. Murray G. Murphey and Elizabeth Flower, *A History of Philosophy in America* (2 vols.; New York, 1977), I, 400.

5. "The emancipation of society from Judaism" is Marx's definition of human freedom. Karl Marx, "On The Jewish Question," in T.B. Bottomore ed., *Karl Marx: Early Writings* (New York, 1964), 40.

6. Richard Hooker, *Works* ed., John Keble (3 vols.; 7th ed., Oxford, 1888), I, 128.

7. Exodus 19:9.

8. Deuteronomy 5:28.

9. Exodus 20:20.

CHAPTER 6

Nebuchadnezzar and the Heroic

It is through the Orphic poet that Emerson brings to light as much of his aspiration to excel in divinity as he dares to do in any of his writings. Recall that Orpheus was a human but Prometheus-like emissary to the nether world. His divine singing, having charmed the gods to relinquish their deathly grip upon Eurydice, Orpheus nearly became the conqueror of death itself. His objective is not in doubt. The song of the Orphic poet, an Emersonian prayer, is a plea for man to become a god.

The Orphic poet is no foolish Israelite. He does not fear his divinity but instead proclaims that man is one. The Orphic poet calls men to assume their rightful place among the gods. This will require that all reverence for the Jews' God come to an end. Emerson cannot be said to have underestimated the seriousness of his purpose. He has carefully seen to it that all danger of looking back has been eliminated. He has taken care not to lose Man Thinking, his Eurydice. Having restored the idea of space to its ancient and pagan identification with time, Emerson's Orphist fears nothing: there is no past at his back for there is no past. "'The oldest chronologies,'" says the Orphic poet at the start of his speech, "'are young and recent.'" There is no necessity to look in any direction but inward, and we know that the most important thing man must study and learn is the self. A good, or "universal man" is a thing of "eternity." *(N,*

CW, I, 42) The overcoming of history, like the putting of nature under foot, is preliminary to becoming a god. In this, Emerson's most outrageous and daring image, the Orphic poet explains why man "'is a god in ruins.'" (Ibid.) He picks a Jewish target.

"'We are, like Nebuchadnezzar,'" says the Orphist, "'dethroned, bereft of reason, and eating grass like an ox.'" (Ibid.) Is it more remarkable that Emerson chose Nebuchadnezzar as a hero or that so little notice has been taken of his having done so? How is it that Emerson calls Nebuchadnezzar a hero, especially on the occasion of that famous tyrant's punishment or ostracism? Emerson's Nebuchadnezzar is condemned to eating grass like an ox because he "applies to nature but half his force....He...is but a half-man,...he is a selfish slave. His relation to nature, his power over it, is through the understanding [only]." (Ibid., 42–3) Appealing as Emerson does so effectively to the element of humanistic romanticism that was in his time, and continues to be today, characteristic of American intellectuals, Emerson assails Nebuchadnezzar as if he were the merest Babylonian bureaucrat. Nebuchadnezzar does not exert his full manhood. Instead he is satisfied with that degree of power over nature and himself that accrues to simple mastery of science and technology. A fallen man, Nebuchadnezzar attempts to bring the universe into line with his own corrupted state. But this wrenches it off its rightful course. Nebuchadnezzar does not exert himself to put nature under foot by means of this reason. Such an exertion, we know, would banish madhouses and swine, would bring men into harmony with each other and all the world. Emerson compares this half-use of human power to the behavior of a timid sovereign. It is, he says, "such a resumption of power, as if a banished king [i.e., Nebuchadnezzar] should buy his territories inch by inch, instead of vaulting at once into his throne." (Ibid., 43)

Emerson, using the romantic attack upon science and technology as bait, here brilliantly makes his point in favor of an heroic Nebuchadnezzar without giving away his ultimate purpose, that is, without stating this purpose outright. He counted on his audiences' indifference to his anti-Jewish vehicle as reasonably he might have done in a community that typically regarded Old Testament Jews as wicked. Subsequent audiences, for whom the choice of Nebuchadnezzar has had as little meaning as the theology he is part of, Jewish or Christian, have been as unmoved by the suggestion of an heroic Nebuchadnezzar as Emerson's contemporaries. Emerson might as well have chosen King Saul. But is this not the genius of revision as it is also the meaning of obviousness, of the idea that something so close to being truer than words can never be said outright? Emerson has placed a shocking fact before his readers but it is an obvious fact or one that is undifferentiated. Emerson does not say what his choice of Nebuchadnezzar *means*. Emerson is a poet of the kind Plato feared, a revolutionary who invites his followers to behold the king alive, as from a balcony, and in custody of his enemies. He does not show them what they know they will soon behold, namely the king's head, ripe from the guillotine, in the hand of a grinning executioner.

But none of this is to say that Emerson's audiences, then or now, failed to sense, however vaguely, the incongruity of Nebuchadnezzar in the role of an heroic "god in ruins." In the same way that contrived incongruity is a source of humor because one knows what the real congruity is, so here the real congruity, which is unstated or obvious, is known by means of the conventional or contrived circumlocutions that suggest it. The Orphist is provocative not reckless. But it is this obvious point in Emerson that we have elaborated in these pages, namely that the explanation of the transhistorical phenomenon of Jewhatred is an obvious, that is, a palpable if packed perception of Judaism. If one wishes to excel in divinity one shall not hesitate to praise Nebuchadnezzar, for this is the man who overcame Judaism in the most profound sense. Nebuchadnezzar destroyed the Temple in 588 B.C. He sacked Jerusalem, the Jews' holy city, and carried the Jews to Babylon where he enslaved them. Nebuchadnezzar as he is known to history and as portrayed in the Book of Daniel is a character of menace and evil. Emerson could scarcely have chosen a more seemingly inappropriate hero unless it were Pharoah himself.

Emerson unpacked or differentiated the obviousness of his choice of Nebuchadnezzar in the privacy of his Notebooks before publishing

Nature. He wrote the following Notebook entry in 1835:

> Why stoops the human race like Nebuchadnezzar to the ground
> & eats grass. Why is it so jealous of its ill fame? Why does it
> resent being told that it is divine. Why so hug its despair & burn
> the blasphemer that declares that not only God was with it but
> God is with it. (JMN, XII, 9)

Certainly this could not be made public. Emerson's reference to
blasphemers burned is too openly an inversion of Daniel, and its
gross anti-Christian component – "so jealous of its ill fame," i.e.,
original sin – would have limited the effectiveness of the Orphist's
speech, compromising the anti-Jewish aspect with a balancing and
too telling anti-Christian one. But this Notebook version, depriving
the published text of *Nature* of its unsayable obviousness, uncovers
the plain meaning of that text. Emerson says that Nebuchadnezzar
was punished with the forfeit of his reason, being turned out to
forage like a beast for the crime of rejecting man's divinity. Emerson
does not stop at this: he claims that ruined man, Nebuchadnezzar in
his banishment, makes martyrs of the sensitive and brave dissenters
and poets who sing of man's divinity and Oneness, hoping in this
way, whatever the risks of torment and persecution at the hands of
pharisaical conformists afraid of truth, to restore man to the god he
is. Emerson's self-portrait of the artist as martyr is modeled certainly
on the record of Jewish martyrdom. But what is the cause of the
martyrdom of the Jews? Naturally the cause is the Jews' opposition
to the doctrine that man is God. What Emerson has given us in
Nature in the speech of an Orphic poet is a perfect reversal of
Judaism by means of a reversal of Nebuchadnezzar as he is known to
history and the Bible.

Of course Nebuchadnezzar was not sent to eat grass like an ox, or
was his reason taken from him because he denied the divinity of man.
Nebuchadnezzar denied no such thing. On the contrary he claimed
that man had the power to be divine in the fundamentally pertinent
sense prohibited by the Second Commandment. Nor is this all.
Emerson's version of Nebuchadnezzar reverses the biblical account
in another equally vital respect. In the Book of Daniel we are told
that when Nebuchadnezzar learned the three Jews, "Shadrach,

Meshach, and Abednego do not...serve my gods, nor worship the golden image which I have set up...," he ordered them "cast...into the midst of a burning fiery furnace."[1] But these Jews are exactly the "blasphemers" Emerson refers to in the Notebook. When we remember that the Jews mentioned here survived a punishment by fire at the hands of idolators just as Abraham did in his encounter with Nimrod mentioned in Chapter 2, the sharpness of Emerson's purpose stands forth brightly indeed. Finally concerning Nebuchadnezzar's being "driven from men,...to eat grass as oxen," this was his punishment, in the biblical source, for idol worship. He was not punished for failing to regard man as divine but the opposite. He denied that "the most High is sovereign over the kingdom of men and gives it to whom he will."[2]

Nebuchadnezzar's conquering of the Jews as part of his divinization signals the defeat of the foolish Israelites. It marks the Emersonian exodus from the world of half-men whose incompleteness is, for Emerson, their clinging to an ill-fame, to their place in between beasts and the divine. Platonic balance or existence in the metaxy is given over to oneness. Hypostatization of the apeirontic, discussed in Chapter 4, here rejects reality on principle in favor of a new man-made reality. In Jewish terms Emerson has assaulted the vital principle of separation (Emerson's hated exclusivity). It is overwhelmed, as was the Holy City by Nebuchadnezzar, in the name of freedom. The Emersonian antagonism to exclusivity is necessarily a replacement of the terrific Jewish Idea. The Jewish principle of separation derives from the core premise that God is One, man is many; Emerson's contrary principle of immanence stems from an opposite ontology. Necessarily the principle of non-separation is also a moral one. The mixing of meat and dairy, of the sabbath and the weekdays, of Jews and all mankind, and of good and evil as well, are implicit in non-separation. Non-separation or Unity, that is, freedom, is itself the Higher Law. Consequently Emerson is at liberty to say, "No law can be sacred to me but that of my nature. Good and bad are but names very readily transferable to that or this; the only right is what is after my constitution, the only wrong what is against it." ("SR", CW, II, 30)

But what can this mean, this reduction of good and bad to names? What effect must this have for the realm of choice or ethics? What does it mean for choosing simply?

We must plumb Emerson's expression beyond its surface appearance as an early form of what is now a characteristic proposition of American relativism or nihilism. It goes deep, to the bedrock in fact, of what has become America's version of freedom and equality born in the years of the national travail over slavery. And, though the abolitionists were the visible midwives of this birth it was Emerson's Mosaic word that nurtured and perfected it for subsequent generations.

How is it, one asks, that "no law can be sacred to me but that of my nature"? Emerson's answer is that the soul simply is. He did in truth discover that "the soul is God."[3] Nature, on the other hand, has two sides, a good and bad, according to Emerson. Is there then a discernible good and evil in nature? Emerson believes there is but in a Pickwickean sense – recall his proud claim that everything was certain for him. Man is nature's creator, nature being the ass upon which Man Thinking, its savior, rides. Emerson has also told us that nature is fluid, not fixed. Or as he also puts it, in nature everything is every other thing. And this is because the "soul appropriates all things." We recall that even hell has its satisfactions, indeed "extreme" satisfactions for Emerson. No single thing is any single thing. If it were, how could the soul appropriate things which are good and bad and still remain good?

When Emerson says that the "good of nature is the soul's" it is a Jonah's soul he has in mind. The soul, he says, is a "swallowing up [of] all relations, parts and times." ("CM", CW, II, 71, 70)

What this all means is that good and bad, the two sides of nature, are precisely those "names" that are very readily transferable to that or this. One may, in other words, reverence the highest – the Ten Commandments – and the lowest – "unhandselled savage nature" such as found in Berserkers and terrible Druids, that is, the opposite of the Ten Commandments, and remain "good." It follows then that "all things are moral" for Emerson.[4]

We have certainly had evidence of what Emerson means by this. It will be useful here to see this same meaning in two of the profoundest disciples of his doctrine of the poet's power in naming good and evil before turning to a consideration of the final and highest purpose that this doctrine served for Emerson. Of these two disciples one was a contemporary – Thoreau – and the other a modern critic and a Jew – Harold Bloom. Both have closely and rightly read the master, Thoreau becoming a maker of his own world almost literally, and Bloom who has adopted a self-described Jewish gnosticism, freely consents that the word and the act are one.

Bloom has most astutely summed up Emerson as one who could prescribe compulsory prayer at Harvard at the same time being a "full brother to the Dionysiac adept who may have torn living flesh with his inspired teeth." This is strong proof of Bloom's boast that he, not Yvor Winters, has read Emerson with greatest acuity.[5] But these impulses of Emerson are not paradoxical or contradictory as Bloom contends, or perhaps pretends. Emerson's two opinions – and, since he did not really go into the woods of Concord there to gaze upon a woodchuck or lynx with a premeditation to devour them, they are opinions or words and not really impulses – are meant to be simply true since the basis for truth is his impulses. More, Emerson's impulses, lacking blood or the hideous reality Bloom describes, also in words, are therefore his own world. They are true absolutely, without need of empirical proof. Emerson does not intend either to literally consume living flesh or to name this impulse evil. He means to show reverence for his opinions that high and low are but names. He does this by naming good and bad after high and low impulses found in his nature as in all men. This naming he calls freedom. There is nothing paradoxical in this.

Bloom's image of the aged Emerson, severe custodian of spiritual forms as well as rankly primitive, is a telling Transcendental index. It is also an index to Bloom's own Transcendentalism and closely follows the typical relationship of poet and critic. In regarding Emerson as paradoxical rather than submitting to the fact of Emerson's paradoxicalness as the substance of his freedom (this making Emerson in a sense beyond criticism), Bloom does not quite completely take Emerson at his word. Thoreau, on the other hand, took Emerson at his word or rather he took Emerson's word to the woods where he became an Emersonian Adam.

In *Walden*'s most Emersonian section, entitled "Higher Laws," Thoreau sets out to prove Emerson's truth that "Our whole life is startlingly moral."[6] Thoreau tells how he discovered Nature's unity. He writes:

> As I came home through the woods with my string of fish,....I caught a glimpse of a woodchuck stealing across my path, and felt a strange thrill of savage delight, and was strongly tempted to seize and devour him raw; not that I was hungry then, except for that wildness which he represented....I found in myself, and still find, an instinct toward a higher, or, as it is named, spiritual life, as do most men, and another toward a primitive rank and savage one, and I reverence them both.[7]

We shall likely never have, from Concord at least, so perfect an expression of Emersonian idealism in practice or so perfect an introduction to Emerson's teaching. Thoreau demonstrates how the Ten Commandments and unhandselled savage nature are both good. If, as Emerson says, "I simply experiment, an endless seeker, with no Past at my back," what better truth is there than the poet's acting upon the echo of his voice which recites the Ten Commandments today, in hard words, and tommorow, in hard words again, contradicts what he said yesterday? A prohibition against tearing living flesh with inspired teeth is among the Bible's first commandments to all men, the so-called Noahide commandments. But has Emerson not said "The Same, the Same" in imitation of Krishna, quoting him to the effect that "'Men contemplate distinctions, because they are stupefied with ignorance....That which the soul seeks is resolution into being above form,...liberation from nature'"? ("P", W, IV, 49, 51)[8]

Final liberation is liberation from nature. But this is the liberation from choice and therefore from selfhood, from "all mean egotism." This is Emerson's final and highest teaching. And the moral aspect, the equal reverencing of high and low impulses, for all its radicalness, is itself only a bait for a much deeper rejection of being as the I that chooses in favor of a unified humanity; that sublime doctrine that there is One Man. Emerson says:

> People represent virtue as a struggle, and take to themselves
> great airs upon their attainments, and the question is
> everywhere vexed, when a noble nature is commended,
> whether the man is not better who strives with temptation. But
> there is no merit in the matter....Why need you choose so
> painfully?...Place yourself in the middle of the stream of power
> and wisdom which animates all whom it floats, and you are
> without effort impelled to truth, to right, and a perfect
> contentment. ("SL", CW, II, 78, 81)

Perfect happiness, then, is the outcome of a man's being faithful to
"himself" if he would shatter ego's kernel, render himself amnesiac,
and struggle, paradoxically, only for unfailing spontaneity. Then
man is free. Only then, moral. As man becomes himself in the midst
of fluid nature, Man is One. "Within man is the soul of the whole;
the wise silence; the universal beauty, to which every part and
particle is equally related; the eternal ONE." ("O-S", CW, II, 160)
As Emersonian freedom binds the self and the collective by
transforming the self into a "we," so Emerson also resolves the
paradox of a freedom that is rooted in the unfreedom of cause and
effect. Freedom, Emerson says, can be liberated by identifying the
will and desire. It is only when man is freedom, at the moment when
he surrenders his will, at the moment when he wraps himself in the
divine cloak and defeats time, at that moment and all moments when
he is creating, that he can live. Judaism, the world's emblem of a
wholly opposite ideal, is the poet's death.

But there is more than an ethical or moral issue involved here.
Emerson's despising of memory and his high hope to merge all wills
in oneness casts him, in spite of all his fancies and abstractions
beyond the realm of sense, back into the arms of physical nature,
although a nature etherealized. It casts him as well into the most
fundamental and telling opposition to Judaism. This is, after all, a
consequence only a god could have avoided. Asking for "insight into
to-day," Emerson says "you may have the antique and future
worlds," but then what is to bind men together? ("AS", CW, I, 67)
Certainly it cannot be language. Emerson is a modern idealist. He

intends to transcend the human condition, time in fact. His object is what Kojève would later describe as the annihilation of man properly so-called; the universal and homogeneous state. It is fascinating then, considering our review of Melian and gnostic exodus in Chapters 1 and 2, to know that the instrument Emerson hit upon as the means to bind men in the new time he envisaged was no ephemeral Plotinian oversoul in the manner of an ancient gnostic but instead a physical thing: blood.

"All men have my blood," he proclaims, "and I have all men's." ("SR", CW, II, 41) To this he adds another point: "The heart in thee is the heart of all; not a valve, not a wall, not an intersection is there anywhere in nature, but one blood rolls uninterruptedly, an endless circulation through all men, as the water of the globe is all one sea, and, truly seen, its tide is one." ("O-S", CW, II, 173–4)

But God does not inhabit mortal veins. We come from a consideration of Emerson's argument that good and bad are but names to a most perfect and perfectly modern identification of the finite with the infinite: of blood with the soul. Emerson turns us from the American Eden or the proposal that God is creation, not creator, to the biblical garden. It is of course in Genesis where the mysterious relationships of creator, of good and evil, and of man receive their Jewish imprint. What are the Jewish meanings and how do they bear upon Emerson's project? We learn the answers to these questions from Emerson's texts, in particular from his misreadings of the Eden story.

Emerson's Orphic poet, drawing upon an Emersonian and biblicized Proclus, describes man's genesis: "Out from him [man] sprang the sun and moon;...the laws of his mind, the periods of his actions externized themselves into day and night, into the year and the seasons." (N, CW, I, 42) Although Emerson's diction approximates that of the Torah, his man creates not out of nothing, but out of Ideas as "uncreated natures." (Ibid., 34) In speaking of these Ideas as "thoughts of the Supreme Being," who is supreme only to the degree that he is the poet or Man Thinking, he revises the biblical passage at the seat of power, the creation out of nothing. He turns to Proverbs to revise its meaning as a means to making his own.[9]

These [Ideas] are they who were set up from everlasting, from
the beginning, or ever the earth was. When he [God] prepared
the heavens, they were there; when he established the clouds
above, when he strengthened the fountains of the deep. Then
they were by him, as one brought up with him. Of them took he
counsel. (Ibid.)

Emerson would have us understand that Moses, an Emersonian
Man Thinking of his time, though he excelled in word-making, had
limited vision and failed to seize his own godhood by "vaulting at
once into his throne." Emerson recreates Moses' time, leading in
biblical terms again to the poetic vision.

There is at this moment for you [mankind] an utterance brave
and grand as that of...the pen of Moses, or Dante, but different
from...these. Not possibly will the soul all rich, all eloquent,
with thousand-cloven tongue, deign to repeat itself; but if you
can hear what these patriarchs say, surely you can reply to them
in the same pitch of voice;...and thou shalt reproduce the
Foreworld again. ("SR", CW, II, 47)

In Moses' own "pitch" Emerson would teach him that his God
"took counsel" from the eternal reservoir of Ideas in the very act of
creation. A poet, a man, is just as much God. Moses failed to see
that his world was his own. And what of man and his creation? Here
we approach the intersection of creation and man, of God's power as
creator or man's, of God's names of good and evil or man's. We find
that Emerson has praise for Adam where God had blame just as
Emerson had blame for the foolish Israelites when God had praise
for them.

Concerning the subject of man's creation, Emerson considers that
man is his own perpetual creator. He is a god eternal in becoming.
"All that Adam had...you have and can do....Build, therefore, your
own world." (N, CW, I, 45) Adam *had* mastery over nature. What
did Adam *do*? He acted to make himself as God. It is these
conditions of Adam's existence that Emerson tells us to emulate. But
new Adam need have no fear of God's punishment; obviously so
since here man is God.

But then man has leave to eat what was forbidden to Adam?

Emerson is astonishingly blunt in answering. He says: "the books which once we valued more than the apple of the eye, we have quite exhausted." ("AS", CW, I, 66) If so who are men to heed? Again Emerson is formidably blunt. He says: "They are the kings of the world who give the color of their present thought to all nature and all art, and persuade men...that this thing which they do, is the apple which the ages have desired to pluck, now at last ripe, and inviting nations to the harvest." (Ibid., 64) Has Emerson not made answer here to the question of the Serpent who asks: "Even if God had said it, should you not eat from all the trees of the garden? For God knows quite well that on the day ye eat thereof, your eyes will be opened and ye will become as gods, knowing what is good and what is evil?"[10]

It is not for nothing that Emerson has called the poet the world's eye. It is the opening of this eye, transparent to permit the "currents of the Universal Being" to course through it, that reveals what is otherwise unseen to ordinary observation. When this eye, "the eye of Reason opens...[then will come] the reverential withdrawing of nature before its God." (N, CW, I, 30) The kings of the world claim the "kingdom of man over nature." (Ibid., 45) And this is of course the kingdom, as Emerson tells us in the final sentence of Nature, that "cometh not with observation," not with seeing, but with the knowledge of good and evil. This event shall summon fallen man to a "dominion such as now is beyond his dream of God." Now shall the Orphist's Nebuchadnezzar vault upon his throne and "enter [his kingdom] without more wonder than the blind man feels who is gradually restored to perfect sight." (Ibid.) This perfect sight, the product of perfect speech or the poet's word made flesh, is what the Serpent promised. He promised peace, an end to all uncertainty. But Emerson's I beholds a vision beyond a dream of God.

Emerson's eye of Reason opens upon a scene of moral relaxation: each has his own perfect circle. It is now clear why he insists there is "no merit" in struggling with temptation. "Why need you choose so painfully" if you may, like Thoreau in the Concord woods, for example, reverence the high and the low equally? Nature's teaching of "indifferency" is in truth the one men must not learn so that, in its place, "the choice of my constitution," the spontaneous choice unvitiated by our will, shall prevail. ("SL", CW, II, 82) Goodness and wisdom are the reward of partaking of the forbidden fruit, not of resisting it. It is not forbidden but rather choice as such that is forbidden. This is how one may "without effort [be] impelled to truth, to right." (Ibid.) But consider the Bible's opposite lesson.

In the Bible man does not acquire God's knowledge of good and evil by eating the forbidden fruit. Man acquires struggle. He is brought to understand good and evil in the human condition as coming from God, no matter what his senses tell him. This is what Emerson rejects. Rather it is what he inverts. Emerson's god, like that of the Jews, is also not seen with the eye of observation. But Emerson's god is "nature." This god is made by the poet. The condition of this god's existence, as we have seen, is a faith that commits men to the rejection and denial of precisely the human condition, of human nature and history, on principle. Emerson's struggle with the God of Israel is a struggle with the biblical text or with the word.

The ancient Jewish text confronts the Emersonian position at its core. Consider the word *tawavaw*, "temptation, delight." The root of this word we are told is "crooked." "If I strive for something that lies out of the path...," explains a 19th century rabbi, a German contemporary of Emerson, "I am...trying to draw a circular line about myself, seeking to enlarge the boundaries of my province, to make myself the center point of a larger circle." This same rabbi, commenting on the word *lehaskeel*, "understanding," as used to describe the promise of knowledge offered by the Serpent (Emerson's eye of Reason), notes in addition that this root is related to

> that which is appropriated exclusively to someone. It is the power which a person has of comprehending the picture of things which flows in through his eyes and adapting them according to himself. This is the person whose perception is too subjective...without testing it with actual reality outside his mind.[11]

Notes

1. Daniel 3:14–15.

2. Ibid., 4:25.

3. Stephen E. Whicher, *Freedom and Fate: An Inner Life of Ralph Waldo Emerson* (Philadelphia, 1953), 21.

4. Emersonians are inclined to argue that this is not a "doctrine of indifferency" or moral relativism ("CM", CW, II, 70). Emerson's text does not support this for it distinguishes what things "preach" from the doctrine of compensation. The former, Emerson says, encourages "indifferency," but not the latter. He means that there must be action above things, above nature.

5. Harold Bloom, *Figures of Capable Imagination* (New York, 1976), 51. Note Ralph Rusk, *The Life of Ralph Waldo Emerson* (New York, 1949), 484, doubts the truth of this story.

6. Henry David Thoreau, *Walden* (New York, 1973), 201.

7. Ibid., 194.

8. Cf. Marion Montgomery, "Emerson and the Emptying of Nature," *Center Journal* 1 (1981), 41: "The dream of indistinguishable *ens* draws Emerson to Krishna."

9. See Proverbs 8:23–30.

10. Genesis 3:1,5.

11. S.R. Hirsch, *The Pentateuch* (5 vols.; 2d ed., rev., Gateshead, England, 1976), I 76–77.

CHAPTER 7

Reconsidering the Jewish Question in Contemporary Scholarship

Aristotle likens the man who would deny the principle of noncontradiction to an object in nature, to a plant.[1] A plant, Aristotle says, cannot distinguish good from evil. Similarly it cannot mark the difference between itself as subject and other things as objects. For it distinctions are ignorance. As for the paradoxes of freedom and necessity, of self-reliance versus the destruction of all mean egotism, Aristotle traced them to the eristical use of language which makes the thinker into the thing thought. The result is an illusory freedom indistinguishable from slavery understood as the death of the human soul. "If...man and that which is thought are the same, man will not be that which thinks, but only that which is thought." And each man's perfect circle becomes every other man's perfect circle, this being the consequence of imposing infinitude upon the finite, of the absolute relativizing of all reality. "If each thing is to be relative to that which thinks, that which thinks will be relative to an infinity of specifically different things."[2] This condition described by Aristotle is the same one that Alexandre Kojève, in the 20th century, identifies as man's freedom, or the equation of thought ("the concept" or C) with temporality (T′) [CT′ or the concept equals temporality].[3]

We may say with confidence that the opposition of Aristotle and Kojève, which expresses all the difference in the world, is not to be resolved empirically for plainly there is only agreement between them at this level. Both apprehend the same reality. Their opposition is philosophic, and concerns man's end and man's beginning. Kojève, whose philosophy is a very nearly definitive weaving together and refinement of Marx and Hegel which also allows for the modifications of Nietzsche and Heidegger, is, at this moment, the quintessential clarification of modern thought. The irreducible premise of this thought is that man is his own creator, atheism. It is for this reason that Kojève rightly insists that man's freedom is man's death, individually and as a species. "If Man is immortal," Kojève says, "there is no freedom." It follows then that "Death and Freedom are but two...aspects of one and the same thing, so that to say 'mortal' is to say 'free.' " He concludes from this, or we may also say that another way of putting this equation is: "where there is *eternal* life and hence God, there is no place for human freedom."[4] One must flee from God almost literally.

This conceptual or philosophic equation of death and freedom is properly to be identified as the major conceptual tradition in American culture from at least the time of Emerson when its first rhetorical and institutional foundations where laid, mainly by the abolitionists. And what was, one hundred and forty years ago, the major conceptual tradition as distinguished from the reality of everyday existence, has become, in our time, the substance of our rhetoric and our institutions.

The contradictions and paradoxes Emerson dealt with in speech have today assumed institutional concreteness. Emerson found the resolution of his paradoxes in the submerging of all mean egotism in the stream of unchoosing, in spontaneity, calling this self-reliance. Freedom is what comes to a human being when at length he is screened from books, from nature and the past, indeed from memory itself. Today the inscrutable contradictions of equality and liberty, of collectivism and anarchy and of all the antinomies characteristic of our civilization, similarly impel an Emersonian resolution above nature. They impel the relinquishment of all mean egotism. We have already mentioned, as a demonstration of this point, the now almost universal relativism and gnosticism of everyday speech. According to this mode of thought each person is the final human authority on all moral questions because he knows, before thought, research or discussion, that all values are equal, i.e., that the good is what is after his constitution.

It is of course not an accident that this development bears an Emersonian stamp which includes our calling this everyday or simplistic relativism openmindedness or toleration. More important, discourse of this type renders each man an I insofar as he is the creator of his own world, while it simultaneously emasculates selfhood by reducing discourse, hence reality, to everyone's own created world. The self is to be replaced by an homogeneous and universal We. In other words, the reducing of all discourse to separate worlds in principle turns language into the discourse of bees or what Kojève calls the definitive destruction of human discourse (CT'). This is tantamount to the identification of one's will and the good, i.e., with what one values. The identification of will and the good, that is to say, the exaltation of spontaneity unhindered by mediation of choice, is equivalent to the destruction of all mean egotism; of selfhood or the I.

The finitude or death of man as the condition of his freedom is an ontological result brought about by his moral freedom, i.e., by his being the author, and not God, of good and evil. Freedom is precisely exodus from the world into a human-world or into the history and culture of which man is the sole maker. What impedes this process of liberation is called slavery. It is in the highest degree relevant that the foremost historical account of slavery in American history and culture equates Judaism with racism and slavery and regards freedom as spontaneity, to be achieved at the most rudimentary non-linguistic level of human life or sex. In no recent work on the subject of American freedom are these points more forcefully made than in *The Problem of Slavery* by David Brion Davis, but the meaning of freedom is hardly more straightforward in Davis than it is elsewhere in contemporary discourse. In fact, the word "freedom" is notoriously suitable to individualist and collectivist uses.[5] Some of freedom's most famous champions, for example, John Stuart Mill and Lord Acton, were remarkable for their suspension or vacillation between collectivist and individualist sentiments.[6] This vacillation is the essence of Davis' understanding of freedom. It is also the soul of modern liberalism, that perpetual oscillation, as Etienne Gilson describes this expression of modern philosophical despair, "between anarchism and collectivism."[7] A review at this point of Davis, the most outstanding historian of freedom, is of great use to the overall goals of this study.

By freedom modern writers commonly mean independence. But independence is both equality (nondependence) and liberty or autonomy ("self-sovereignty"). Freedom understood in this way is then a reflection of the founding doctrine of modern political theory, the so-called state of nature. Freedom, that is to say, is a term of contradictory or opposed meanings because man himself is considered to be a being without a being, a being that is free. This can be said in another way – viz., that man's being is historical.

It is due to the perception of human being as historical that modern political life and theory have been called "an internecine struggle among ideological outgrowths of the modern historical consciousness."[8] The conditions of freedom are, for modern thinkers, historical. More exactly, freedom is a return to the state of nature, whether within history (Rousseau) or by means of it (Marx, Kojève).[9] In other words, the context of modern history is freedom because the context of modern freedom is historical.

For Kojève (as for Marx and Hegel) historicism is true or proper philosophy because, to use Kojève's Hegelian terminology, the Concept is Time or History, CT. This means that the processes of History which transcend temporality have replaced philosophy and its hitherto transcendental objects. But liberals, maintaining that the concept is mere temporality, CT', or that all meaning is in the present, destroy philosophy, that is, history properly understood. As Kojève correctly says, "this (skeptical) type of thought makes all philosophy impossible by denying the very idea of truth."[10] In fact, liberalism or vulgar historicism relativizes absolute relativism or philosophic historicism. In doing so it appears to doubt the absolutism of Marx or of Kojève along with what all moderns are agreed in calling the absolutism of classical philosophy and Western religion or monotheism. The liberal doubts the radical claim to absolute knowledge, that is, to knowledge of history's end or meaning.

But there is, as perhaps the reader has already detected, a great irony here. The liberal position is actually a radicalization of radicalism and thereby a fulfillment of it. The claim of CT', that the concept is temporal, waives or suspends the principle of noncontradiction and asserts that all truth is relative to time and place absolutely. But this is the realm of freedom or the goal of Kojève's posthistorical man.

> Man becomes an animal again...after the end of History. [Then] men would construct their edifices and works of art as birds build their nests and spiders spin their webs, would perform musical concerts after the fashion of frogs and cicadas....But there is more...[:] the definitive disappearance of human Discourse (*Logos*) in the strict sense. Animals of the species *Homo sapiens* would react by conditioned reflexes to vocal signals or sign "language," and thus their so-called "discourses" would be like what is supposed to be the "language of bees". [To this statement of Kojève, itself one of the most honest and straightforward assertions of radicalism in print he adds the following historical observation.] From a certain point of view, the United States has already attained the final stage of Marxist "communism."...[T]he "American way of life"...[is] the type of life specific to the post-historical period, the actual presence of...the "eternal present."[11]

Davis' ontological and moral positions are founded in contradiction, actually in the denial of the principle of noncontradiction. The effect of this should be that Davis, like Cratylus, may only move his finger. Certainly he should refrain from making moral judgments. But because Davis' abrogation, like Emerson's, of the principle of noncontradiction is, in its ethical dimension, precisely what he means by freedom and "uniform justice," he does not limit himself to a movement of his finger. As for moral judgments, Davis' study is nearly overwhelmed by them. His identification of the gnostic and bloodthirsty 16th century Muntzerites, and similar groups friendly to holy murder, as "the first abolitionists" is telling.[12] These were in truth the first abolitionists but in a sense opposite to the one Davis supposes.

We learn why Davis praises such astonishingly implausible types by understanding his confusion and vacillation between a related admiration for the freedom of individuality, of "self-sovereignty," and an equally strong affection for a contrary impulse among abolitionists in favor of the all-powerful and universal state. The first abolitionists grasped the need to end "possessive individualism," that is, they realized that the solution to the intolerable contradictions of their position, or Davis', can be found only in the elimination of selfhood and its replacement by spontaneity that shall bypass the limiting conventions of property and monogamy.

By exposing slavery in "all...acts of dominion" Davis spares nothing in the way of emphasis or historical example.[13] Dominion includes not only the acts "that virtually re-enslaved the American blacks after the Civil War," but also "all the subtle strategems, passive as well as aggressive...all the interpersonal knots and invisible webs of ensnarement which are so much a part of the psychopathology of our everyday lives."[14] More, slavery may in principle "be applied to wives and children in a patriarchal family."[15] In sum, slavery is the "perfect antithesis of individual autonomy or self-sovereignty."[16] The "dream of a more perfect society," of true and complete self-sovereignty, stands against all "traditional authority," all "accepted norms," all "conventional society." Freedom is the opposite of society and all dominion as we know it. It is simply "the timeless categories of nature" versus "civilization," or the return to the state of nature.[17] Naturally Davis is concerned about etatisme. Is there not in Hegel, who has been explained to him by Kojève, an "infatuation with the...all-powerful state"?[18] Not doubting that the dominion of a state, certainly an all-powerful, universal and homogeneous one, must be a "facet of subordination" no less grave than an interpersonal knot, Davis expresses puzzlement about the tendency of his idea of freedom to veer toward state dominion. Davis is ambivalent about Rousseau as well.

Tracing the intellectual origins of antislavery thought to the great Genevan, Davis writes: "Because Rousseau addressed himself to the emancipation of all mankind, and because he had no faith in...gradual progress or a return to the state of nature, he...[favored] subjection to the General Will." Davis considers this a "paradox": Does liberty or "genuine liberation...[mean] a higher form of servitude?" Perhaps it is only a matter of opinion "whether one" sees the general will "as democratic or totalitarian."[19] When Davis considers the matter of freedom from the standpoint of the "emancipation of all mankind...[and] the ancient dream of a more perfect society," its collectivist imperatives are clear to him. The totalitarian aspects fade. If self-sovereignty is to be an uprooting of self and personality, (collective freedom), there is need for the self-sovereignty of the state.

But it is also true that Davis' approval of centralized state power, actually of the universal and homogeneous state, is typically hedged with the confusion and embarrassment that liberals evince in their admiration for Communist totalitarianism and their despising of so-called fascism or undemocratic regimes. (Again Kojève is particularly refreshing in this regard and quite correctly understands that both Communist and "rightwing" or fascist regimes are democratic.)[20] That Davis should actually be an opponent of progressive government or centralization, adopting a so-called libertarian position (or the position of simple-minded anarchism that fails to understand itself as ultimately favoring the elimination of mean egotism), is hardly to be expected. Centralization as the means for self-sovereignty is exactly what he favors. Thus Davis expresses the opinion of liberal historiography that the failures of the American Revolutionary generation can be traced to those "fears and suspicions...[of] the Federal Constitution" that prevented an initial defense of individual liberties. One must recall, he says, "the vehement opposition to Hamilton's modest experiments with centralized planning...to begin to appreciate the distance between the ideal of emancipation and its effective implementation."[21] And, when self-sovereignty is liberation from the self or collective freedom, it is not just any state that will be adequate. Only the all-powerful universal and homogeneous state can implement self-sovereignty. In sum, Davis seeks self-sovereignty, but he fears the state. He seeks collective freedom and welcomes the state. These confusions are not only theoretical, but affect the narrative level as well where they appear in the form of factual inaccuracies.

Davis is fascinated with collective liberty and seeks its heroes in the historical record. George Wallace, a mid-18th century Scottish jurist, was a promising expounder of the "radical implications" of collective freedom who "denounced American slave laws as contrary to the law of nature. Significantly, he explicitly rejected the theory of possessive individualism....Wallace's principles presented a direct challenge to established authorities....Governmental sanction... served only to show the illegitimacy of government."[22] But Davis has not himself fully appreciated the radical implications of collective freedom. It appears that Wallace, like Hegel, had no wish to sanction the illegitimacy of quite all government. His radicalism, Davis observes in a footnote, "was based on the superior right of the state."[23] Similarly, one William Fox, whom Davis judges to have been "an unusually radical abolitionist," combined a zeal for the emancipation of French Negroes with a prepossession for "bringing them under the protection and control of government."[24]

Davis finds the friends of freedom among anarchists and collectivists, and among friends and foes of Southern slavery. He ties the name of Mikhail Bakunin to that of William Lloyd Garrison, calling him a "champion...of individual liberty."[25] The juxtaposition is richly revealing. Bakunin, an anarchist and originally a Hegelian, indulged a hatred for Marx that was doctrinal as well as personal. Equally consuming was Bakunin's doctrinal and personal hatred for Jews, the symptomatic passion of mankind's liberators.[26]

The contradictory pronouncements and vacillations of Davis on the subjects of freedom, the self and the state cannot fail to invade his work at all levels, in particular at the methodological and ethical levels. If it is the case that "one generation...[is not] endowed with greater moral insight than...another," so that it takes "unusual objectivity to see that an alien society is neither more innocent nor more wicked than one's own," then we should reasonably expect Davis to regard all presents as equal, neither praising nor blaming.[27] But Davis, praising and blaming excessively, also supposes his present is superior to all others.

The moral equality of cultures has as its methodological corollary the principle of presentism or relativism: each present is the equal of every other present. Although this has long been a staple of liberal historiography, its superficiality is more plausible than its longevity. Presentism suggests that history is always interpretation or relativistic, that each present is bound by its own ideas so that the past must be a product of the present's vision. In this sense all presents are equally unfree and equally ignorant of history or of any knowledge. But this view, a form of CT', is not simply contradictory. One could not judge the past or even reach it if presentism were true because no understanding of the past as past would ever be possible. This, after all, is what Davis commits himself to in his principle of objectivity. But Davis does judge the past and also claims to know it. More, he claims moral superiority regarding the past, its ideas and leaders. The key to all these confusions in Davis is to be found, as we know, in his ideal of freedom as a doctrine of spontaneity.

The gnostic revolutionaries of the 16th century whom Davis considers the "first abolitionists" were among the initial discoverers of collective freedom because they realized that freedom is the expression of man's "deepest desires," actually of desire simply.[28] Collective freedom, in other words, is at length the equality of all desires, and therein the eradication of choice among desires. The significance of this ultimate goal or resolution of the contradictions that beset Davis' position is revealed in connection with his application of presentism in the ethical realm. Although objectivity will not permit Davis to praise or blame, it is in his contradictory position as absolute moralist that the character of his idealism is clearest.

As Davis' present is superior to the pasts of others and free where others' are bound, so, his principle of objectivity, resting upon the moral equality of cultures, is a warrant for ethical discourse. Moreover, in view of Davis' understanding of freedom as cultural relativism, one might expect, if Davis is to praise and blame at all, that he will praise tribal particularities and not universalist principles when he finds them. But Davis does not intend to be caught in the dilemmas or paradoxes of anarchy and collectivism but to resolve them or, more correctly, he intends to embody their resolution. Significantly he praises the expression of desire and deplores the restraint of it or choice. Davis celebrates liberated cultures and condemns rational ones; in particular he praises Africa and, *mutatis mutandis*, the "Third World." He systematically opposes the West, Christianity, Judaism, all of which demonstrate the "arrogant ethnocentrism" of those who believe transcendent truths.[29]

As Davis approaches the heart of the liberal project, of radical atheism and finitude elaborated by Kojève and expressed by Davis at the level of narrative, we learn that the conflict of "human rights and property rights" is the ultimate clue to the contradiction of slavery.[30] The "treatment of man as property dramatized the moral dilemmas of the [Enlightenment] age." This age is for Davis the turning point in the history of man's freedom.[31]

The conflict between property rights and human rights is, like presentism, a staple of liberal as well as of Marxist discourse. Also, like presentism, this conflict has its roots in the fundamental suppositions of Davis' vision of freedom. There is, of course, no conflict between human and property rights. Rather, this conflict is an expression of the principle that the concept is temporal (CT'). The conflict of human rights and property rights is nothing more than human relationships conceived in context of valuelessness, a transformation of a question about the good into a question to be decided without reference to it. This transformation from the context of justice to so-called "fairness" or utilitarianism goes to the root of what Davis understands by freedom.

In context of the suppositions that ideas are historical artifacts and all cultures are equal, the matter of property is something more than an element of anticapitalist rhetoric. Property is of the essence of possessive individualism and the nodal point of slavery. Human rights on this view are antecedent to property and antithetical to it. Just as Rousseau considered selfishness to be the result of the division of labor arising with the discovery of meum et teum, of property, so Davis considers freedom, that is, collective freedom or the relinquishment of the possessed self, as the resolution to the contradiction of slavery. The freedom of the collective self is that gnostic freedom which, Davis says, reflected a "changed view of history."[32] The first abolitionists, the Muntzerites, made "it possible to identify virtue with man's deepest desires, and sin with the inhibition and repressive forces blocking the path to the [worldly] millennium."[33] Here then is freedom, contradiction's reward.

That particular desire, acted upon without a self or the mediation of thought or inhibition, is above all the sexual desire. But liberation regarding sex is not an arbitrary ideal. The elimination of that most resistant, seemingly natural (i.e., not historical or man-made) division of labor or the division between men and women in the production of the race is freedom of a high order, what Kojève refers to as love-making "as adult beasts." In love-making as adult beasts, the human animal achieves the animal's "sentiment of self" but without being plagued with the "I," created by desire, to possess another desire. A beast is aware only of desire and its satisfaction. It knows nothing either of its object as another "I" or of the consequences of love-making. The exposition of African slavery in Davis as mere narrative is a reflection of the points refined with great care in Kojève.

The occasion for Davis to propose his ethical and methodological principles that other cultures are not more wicked or innocent than one's own is his discussion of Africa. Africans, says Davis, "permitted the open expression of many impulses that had long been sublimated in Europe." For example, Africans "did practice human sacrifice, and...large numbers of slaves were sometimes killed at religious ceremonies....[Also] people...mutilated their bodies and drank human blood, and...kings...lived in palaces decorated by thousands of human skulls."[34] But Davis, whose volumes are laden with contempt for the West and for Christianity as equivalents to enslavement, has no scorn for Africa. What is more, he is obliged to argue that activities of the type he defends among the Africans were not understood by contemporary Europeans, although he understands them. Moreover, while "even the most perceptive [European] observers were incapable of appreciating the African's highly complex picture of the supernatural world, the significance of his rituals, the richness of his mythology," Davis' own perception is not limited to these aspects.[35] This perception enjoins a further praise or indulgence of African religion and a distaste, even what seems a hatred, for the rituals of Christianity (which did not include human sacrifices or drinking of blood, as a matter of fact). On what principle does Davis withhold a negative judgment of the African picture of the supernatural while applauding the overthrow of the "collective superego" in Europe?[36]

The answer is sex. The Africans, says Davis, were free in this all-important area.

> There can be no doubt that many African cultures made sex a prominent and publicly acknowledged part of life....The most popular god in several West African cultures was a fun-loving prankster and wanderer who was free to take any woman, and whose erotic impersonations...shocked...Europeans. Negro girls received...a well-planned sexual education, which included elaborate exercises and prolonged stimulation of the appropriate organs.[37]

Europeans, says Davis, could not accept this "challenge to conventional standards." They could not be reconciled to the "obvious and shocking fact that Africans enjoyed sex and were unashamed." Although the Europeans are objects of scorn for Davis because of their supposed bondage to class interests and economic factors, the Africans are praised by him for their frank and unashamed sexuality. Europeans he calls "sneaking hypocrites," but the Africans were unashamed.[38]

What appears to be arbitrary or even racialist moralizing here is, in fact, the application of Davis' doctrine of freedom in its ethical dimension. His choice of Anabaptists as the first abolitionists explains how he comes to his concern for sexual freedom.

The Muntzerites, also admired by Marx, were among the purest exponents of gnostic millennialism in the early modern period. Supposing that freedom was disembodied desire ("soul"), Muntzer considered everything that held desire in check, all matter in fact, as evil. Communism in property and wives, or collective freedom, was his objective. It was to be achieved by an annihilation of ego, or selflessness. He considered this object the sign of liberty. It was his great hope, as Davis says, to "liberate himself from sin, annihilate evil." And Davis does not deny that this led "at times" to "slaughtering the children of darkness."[39] (Muntzer himself enjoyed beheading his enemies personally.)

Typically, Davis does not reconcile this conflict of sovereignties. Instead he praises the Muntzerian

> faith in man's will and the power of love,...their hostility to all compromise and rationalization, and...determination to wage unremitting war against the forces of darkness...[because they saw the great truth that an] attack on slavery could easily develop into a challenge to law, government, and institutional restraints of every kind....[They saw that] arguments against empty conventions, prescriptive rights, and the alienation of liberty, were as applicable to society in general [i.e., to society as such] as to the most tyrannical form of servitude.[40]

Of course, the kingdom of darkness to which the Muntzerites referred was Christianity, in particular, the doctrine of sin and the idea of evil. Davis also deplores the idea of sin, an element he did not find in African religion. He notes that the "essence of both sin and slavery was a denial of self-sovereignty."[41] In his identification with the Muntzerites the several contradictory strands of Davis' understanding of freedom and slavery begin at last to join coherently. The great principle upon which freedom as an absolute is reared, or CT' according to which all values are equal, is none other than the principle of Muntzer and the gnostic revolutionaries Davis admires as the harbingers of modern freedom. Their principle holds that man is beyond good and evil. In the religious language of the 16th century, gnostic men who are elevated in this way were said to be perfect. For this reason, they may indulge their deepest desires and be free. In Davis' description of the Ranters (a remarkably selective description, suggesting at times a rather elfin picture of this often criminal group), Davis explains in Emersonian language how they regarded sin as "but...a name that could be made meaningless by an act of will." In this way the Ranters showed there could be "no justification for inequalities of sex and property which violated the law of spontaneous love."[42] Spontaneous love, or desiring without the inhibition of choice or thought, is the object of sexual liberty and the community of wives. These are in truth the means to an uprooting of possessive individualism. Moreover, the liberation of man from sin is precisely the liberation from the ego that fears death and experiences it as a material being. It is also therefore liberation from all distinctions whatsoever; it is collective freedom. And what of God?

The Muntzerites overthrew the collective superego. Themselves they considered new Adams. But it was the God of the Jews, and by extension the Christian church, that Muntzer and his fellow revolutionaries considered the enemy, the collective superego that must be overthrown. Having forced man to choose between the law of God and their deepest desires or freedom, God then punished men for having made the wrong choice, although it was God and not men who understood why some particular tree should be different from all others. Muntzer's aspiration was to rise above the distinction between good and evil as established outside man, and thereby to liberate man from evil and from sin, to "annihilate evil" as Davis puts it. But the elevation of man beyond good and evil, or the equality of all values which permits man to say that good and bad are whatever he makes them, is absolute knowledge, the divine vantage point. The quest for the good is over.

God's punishment is death to the man who attempted to rise above good and evil. In overcoming God, the new Adams must overcome death. More precisely, man must overcome death at God's hand. This man can do by suicide or precisely by killing the soul as an immortal thing outside of his control. Freedom, in other words, calls for the death of God, for the most complete atheism and this calls for man's death, for his mortality. It is in this context that we are to understand Davis' praise of Africa and his attack on Western religion and on the West generally. The "testing grounds of Christianity" came in the Enlightenment when Christianity had to turn from an obscurantist concern with souls to a devotion to "social justice."[43] But Judaism as origin of both monotheism and the "moral absolutism" of "Biblical particularism" is slavery in its essence.[44]

Notes

1. Aristotle, *Metaphysics*, 1006a15.

2. Ibid., 1011b10–12.

3. Alexandre Kojève, *Introduction to the Reading of Hegel, Lectures on the Phenomenology of Spirit* (New York, 1969), 101–102

4. Ibid., 250, 247, 258.

5. David Brion Davis, *The Problem of Slavery in Western Culture; The Problem of Slavery in the Age of Revolution* (Ithaca, New York, 1966, 1975).

6. The case of Mill is well known. On Acton see E.D. Watt, " 'Freedom' as an Incantation: The Example of Lord Acton," *The Journal of Politics*, 25 (1963), 461–471.

7. Etienne Gilson, "Concerning Christian Philosophy, The Distinctiveness of the Philosophic Order," in Raymond Klibansky and W.J. Paton, eds., *Philosophical and Historical Essays Presented to Ernst Cassirer* (New York, 1963), 68.

8. William Galston, *Kant and the Problem of History* (Chicago, 1975), 4.

9. Kojève, *Introduction*.

10. Ibid., 102. Of course, this condition, CT′, is also the condition of human freedom at the end of history, according to Kojève. See below.

11. Ibid., 159–161n5.

12. Davis, *The Problem of Slavery*, I, 299.

13. Ibid., II, 564.

14. Ibid.

15. Ibid., I, 31.

16. Ibid., II, 264.

17. Ibid., I, 12, 69, 12.

18. Ibid., II, 563.

19. Ibid., I, 415.

20. Kojève, *Introduction*, 160n5: "The democratization of...Germany...by way of Hitlerism." Although it is well understood that what Fackenheim calls "ideological fanaticism," or the identification of truth and the movement of history, is totalitarian, e.g., Communism or Nazism, it is supposed that liberalism, characteristically posed as moderate and tolerant between the "extremes of left and right," is the modern antidote to fanaticism. In fact, liberalism is modern fanaticism in nuce or radicalism radicalized which on occasion breaks out in its right and left forms. What else is liberalism but the "futility of everything that is an end in itself," Hannah Arendt's description of Nazism quoted by Fackenheim against ideological fanaticism? Fackenheim, *Metaphysics and Historicity* (Milwaukee, Wisconsin,1961), 6.

21. Davis, *The Problem of Slavery*, II, 257.

22. Ibid., 269, 270.

23. Ibid., 269n21.

24. Ibid., 381.

25. Ibid., 263.

26. On Engels see ibid., 468. His study of English workers is "one of the greatest of antislavery tracts."

27. Davis, *The Problem of Slavery*, I, 467.

28. Ibid., 299, 297.

29. Ibid., II, 47.

30. Ibid., 268.

31. Ibid., 263.

32. Ibid., I, 296.
33. Ibid., 296–297. Also "internal impulse," 299.
34. Ibid., 467–468.
35. Ibid., 467.
36. Ibid., 297.
37. Ibid., 469.
38. Ibid., 470.
39. Ibid., 297.
40. Ibid., 299, 414.
41. Ibid., 292.
42. Ibid., 298. This entire section of Davis' study, lacking any reference to the important work of Eric Voegelin and expressing the most exaggerated and inaccurate portrayal of the "first abolitionists," is most astonishing. It seems at times almost to be propaganda for the principle of terrorism. He speaks, for example, of "symbolic acts of violence". 297.
43. Ibid., 337. See also 303, 306.
44. Ibid., II, 536.

CHAPTER 8

Freedom and the Jewish Idea

Davis' charge against Judaism is the most serious one a defender of modern freedom can make. Judaism is "racism" and this is slavery. Here then is the "new language" Bauer promised for the ancient and transcendent reality of Jewhatred. And, like Emerson's Man Thinking, Davis discovers that freedom calls upon him to misread biblical texts precisely to show how Judaism places "Biblical authority above abstract and uniform justice."[1] It is the purpose of biblical law, Davis thinks, to preserve Jewish "racial purity."[2] Judaism is then the very worst sort of particularism and slavery known to a scholar of Davis' time, it is racism. Davis' charges are in truth more astonishing than the outwardly more shocking comparison of Stanley Elkins, mentioned before. Davis' comments on Judaism have occasioned no comment at all. This is significant in several respects. We note here only the methodological aspect and suggest there is more than a coincidental connection between the silence of reviewers and, presumably, publisher's readers, regarding Davis' equation of Judaism with racism and slavery and the inaccuracies of his account of Jewish subjects. The connection is that where values and presents are equal, facts become interpretations. Davis' practical denial of fact, that is of history, is theoretically identical to Emerson's hatred of memory.

Placing his attack upon Judaism in context of the Enlightenment prejudice favoring universalism against particularism[3] (that is, in context of modern freedom), Davis' comments on Judaism are the following. Davis' claim that "no Biblical legislation prohibited the beating or maltreatment of bondsmen, though a Jewish owner might be liable to punishment if his slave died within three days of a severe chastisement" is typical of his scholarship on this subject.[4] The statement is a web of falsehoods. To begin, the passage Davis cites (Exodus 21:20–21) is found only five lines before the well-known reference that Jews must free slaves who have been mistreated. Further, Davis has paid no heed to Jewish sources, including the Bible, but has relied on secondary writers, in particular Isaac Mendelsohn. He is ill-served by Mendelsohn on this occasion.

The matter of a slaveholder's liability Davis takes almost verbatim from Mendelsohn whose account is incorrect in two particulars.[5] First, Exodus 21:20–21 is universally understood in Jewish sources to mean that a slave who lived one (not three) days after mistreatment by the slaveholder was not to be "avenged" (the Bible's term). If the slave survived mistreatment the owner was punished according to Exodus 21:26–7. But this is not the most important correction of Mendelsohn. Jewish law based on the passage cited by Davis involved the following points. A slave who is mistreated (as distinguished from being reproved with a rod), that is, who is attacked by the owner with some instrument other than a rod or even with a rod for a purpose other than to reprove, and who dies as a result of this mistreatment – no matter when – is a victim of murder. The slave is to be avenged. In other words, the passage covers the case of lawful chastisement of a slave which, should it end in the death of the slave (a possibility the Bible considers farfetched) must be punished as prescribed. Moreover, this specific set of principles applies only to the slaveholder. The murder of a slave is murder.

Davis also fails to take into account the several authorities on slavery such as Maimonides who notes that non-Jewish slaves, those to be treated "with rigor," must be well-fed, even eating from the master's table. Slaves were not to be embarrassed or spoken to in a raised or angry voice as matters of Jewish law.[6] As for the suggestion of Jewish racism in this case, i.e., that one who mistreated a slave "might be liable to punishment," it is simply ludicrous. The citation itself is the best proof. It says a slave is to be "avenged," that is, *nakom yenakame*; the slaveholder must be beheaded. But Davis attempts to sustain the charge of racism and moral absolutism in other ways.

Davis insists that Jewish enslavement of the Canaanites was racist. Actually the Jews were charged to exterminate the Canaanites who, learning of this, tricked the Jews into enslaving them instead. Race had nothing to do with the matter and, indeed, a Canaanite slave was required to observe large parts of Jewish law, including circumcision, the sign of the covenant. Unless this were so a Jewish master would not be permitted to free a slave to make a congregation of ten males.[7] But the charge of racism and absolutism is also said by Davis to attach to Jewish laws and customs regarding marriage, i.e., to sexual matters.

Concerned that the abolitionists "apparently assumed that the evil of divorce was more self-evident than the evil of slavery," Davis chides the abolitionists for failure "to mention...the right of a [Jewish] bridegroom to have his bride stoned to death if her father could not produce the 'tokens' of her virginity."[8] Undoubtedly the contrast between Davis' indulgence (actually, praise of African sexuality and liberation) and his comments here is stark. Leaving aside the matter of the "bridegroom's rights" (they apply in the context of the period from betrothal to marriage, about a year, and the "tokens" would include two witnesses to the act of adultery), it is relevant that the Jews did consider the evil of divorce and unchastity as evident as slavery. Even supposing the wrongfulness of Jewish law on this matter, why, on Davis' principle of objectivity, can we not suppose the Jews were not more wicked than the Africans or more innocent? The answer, we know, is freedom. Yet, the fact is that Jewish laws have nothing to do with racial purity but entirely to do with idolatry.

The enslavement of the Canaanites, the prohibition against marriage to non-Jews, as well as laws regarding virginity, all go to the heart of the difference between Davis and Judaism and, ultimately, between Davis and the entire Western heritage. It is the difference between idolatry and freedom as the Bible understands it. The Canaanites symbolize idolatry; they are not a racial group. Idolatry, we have already noted, is the most serious crime in the Bible where it is the counter to monotheism. As idolators Canaanites are slaves by definition; indeed, one might say they are slaves by nature in the sense that idolatry runs with the grain of human imagination and not against it. Slavery in the Jewish context is precisely idol worship, the condition of the Jews at Sinai when they turned to worship the golden calf. The objective of rooting Canaanites out of Israel, the land the Jews had been instructed to inhabit, is exactly redemption: in a word, freedom.

Davis does not make clear if he understands that the identification of "sin and slavery" is in reality the choice between monotheism and reason on the one hand and atheism and desire on the other. Kojève, however, is eminently clear on the point. But Kojève's clarity is not greater than Emerson's, whose attack upon the "foolish Israelites" in "Self-Reliance" is a precise identification of sin and slavery. It is an identification of freedom with the gravest sin or idolatry.

In "Self-Reliance", the essay of "foolish Israelites" published in 1841, five years after *Nature*'s Orphic annunciation concerning the coming divinity of man, Emerson makes the following proclamation: "I would write on the lintels of the door-post, *Whim*." ("SR", CW, II, 30) This sentence revises two related Jewish symbols of freedom. As in the case of his misreading of Exodus in the same essay, Emerson again reverses the combined and the separate meaning of the two sentences he draws upon. Emerson's revision involves in the main two biblical passages. The first of these, Exodus 12:22–23, concerns the instructions to the Jews about the Passover and escape from Egypt. In Exodus the Jews are told to "touch the lintel and the doorposts with the blood [of the Paschal lamb]....For the Lord will pass through to slay the Egyptians; and when he sees the blood on the lintel and the two doorposts, the Lord will pass over the door," destroying the firstborn of the Egyptians only.[9] The second passage called up by Emerson's mining of the Jewish Bible is from Deuteronomy. Just as the passover and exodus leading to Sinai are the chief symbolic events in Jewish liturgy, the *Sh'ma* [Hear], as it is called, is the Jews' statement of creed regarding these events. These passages embody what Emerson calls the "terrific Jewish Idea."

The second passage or *Sh'ma*, "Hear [O Israel, the Lord is your God, the Lord is One]," recited during morning and evening prayer and also upon retiring, is the first sentence of a section of the prayerbook taken largely from Deuteronomy. Of all sacred Jewish writings, it is the most important from a ritual standpoint and the most provocative from an Emersonian one. It is almost the word made flesh. In the *Sh'ma* the Jew is instructed to place it, the *Sh'ma* "on the doorposts of your house and on your gates." The contents of the *Sh'ma* unambiguously affirm what precedes it, the decalogue and its terms, the covenant, according to which the Jews promise to obey the Torah, these same "commandments and statutes." The first of these commandments is "I am the Lord your God who brought you out of the land of Egypt, from the house of bondage." As for the *Sh'ma*, it concludes with the warning to "remember and do all my commands...for...I am the Lord, who brought you forth out of the land of Egypt."[10] The *Sh'ma* comprehends a logical whole beginning and ending with the central Jewish assertion, or Emerson's "terrific Jewish Idea" that God is One. Inside the *Sh'ma* is contained the instruction to learn the statement itself and what it instructs, namely that the Jew must observe the "statutes and commandments," the Torah, as part of the covenant, including the *Sh'ma* and, returning to the starting or first principle, the message it contains; that God is One. Thus the Jew obeys the First Commandment – I am the Lord your God who brought you out of the land of Egypt. Since the commandment is actually a declarative not an imperative sentence we are to understand that acknowledgement constitutes obedience, specifically, acknowledgement that it was God that performed the liberation from Egypt, this act being as it were a definition of God.

God's oneness and the Exodus are integrated conceptually and thematically as is the language of Exodus and Deuteronomy which describes this relation. Emerson, by collapsing the language of both passages into one sentence, reformulates the relationship of exodus and divinity. Consider to begin that there is no writing on the lintels or on the doorposts in the Exodus passage, rather blood is splashed.

The observer of this sign is God, not men; certainly it is not Emerson or "I". In the Deuteronomy passage, the *Sh'ma* is written but only on the doorposts, not on the lintels. However, Emerson "would *write* on the *lintels.*" Emerson's reversals ramify coherently – lintels for doorposts, writing for blood, exodus for *Sh'ma*, Whim for specificity as to firstborn and Jews, Emerson for God.

Once it is understood that whim has at least two meanings as a matter of fact – whim as caprice, and as the antonym of *Sh'ma* (thus a precise meaning) – it next appears that whim has two more meanings, each implicit in the primary meanings appearing at the surface. One is that whim is a pun. A pun is a word (here whim itself) with two meanings. Whim is also a machine used to mine ore or draw water, more common in Emerson's time than presently. What is the pun, supposing the mining of Jewish lore is the second meaning? The Jewish letter *shin* resembles a *W*, the first letter of the word Shaddai (a name of God), frequently the only letter printed on the container (mezuzah) holding the *Sh'ma* when placed on the doorposts of a Jewish home. The remainder of the word Whim, or him, is suggestive of a disparagement of the name usually appearing, at the same time referring playfully, half seriously, to himself; the poet.

One cannot press this sort of speculation. It is risky. But in addition to support in the text itself, there are certain factors in Emersonian scholarship and in Emerson that lend credibility to these speculations. For example, Rusk assures us that "Self-Reliance" "had been longest in [Emerson's] mind."[11] There is also the consideration that Emerson's love of word play, visible in his Notebooks as well as in his published writings, was excessive. As to how extensively Emerson knew Jewish lore, it is an open question. He had surely seen mezuzot when he passed through "the Jews' quarter" of an Italian town in 1833. (JMN, IV, 181) As for Emerson's personal dislike for Jews as people it was, if not excessive, certainly typical. But Emerson especially disliked Judaism and knew why he did. Consideration of the ritual language of the *Sh'ma*, "the terrific Jewish Idea," is vital to comprehending Emerson's revision of this idea.

The *Sh'ma* is remarkable in Jewish observance in the way that it becomes an object in the course of being observed, *viz.*, the parchment is boxed and attached to doorposts and, in phylacteries, bound daily upon the arm and placed upon the head of male Jews in morning prayer. (Deuteronomy 5:8, "thou shalt bind them [i.e., these words] for a sign upon thine hand, and they shall be as frontlets between thine eyes.") The words thus become things; indeed very nearly flesh. In their use as objects, and especially in being placed next to the heart, the *Sh'ma* is a caricature of Emerson's enterprise. Of course the encroachment upon thinghood, considered from the Jewish standpoint, emphasizes the dreadful import of the "name." The word to be placed "upon your heart" is that God is One, that is, the *Sh'ma*. This exercise is intended to promote a meaning the opposite of Emerson's, wherein the objectification of words in the wearing of them becomes an index to the sanctity of the One. The wearing of phylacteries is intended to be a humbling experience, even terrifying, for the Jew, even as Emerson's exaltation of the divinity of eloquence (an object the reverse of that served by phylacteries), is conceived to raise up and embolden Man Thinking.

Whatever Emerson knew of Hebrew and of the Jews, and he knew something about both, he knew English well. Whim does not mean lawful, regular, devout, constant. All of these meanings, the reverse of whim, apply to the *Sh'ma*. Furthermore, while the *Sh'ma* is about God and the central Jewish proposition that God's oneness is rooted in the exodus, whim is notoriously not one. Of whim's several meanings, one of these, pun, requires, as noted already, that it have at least two. *One* in its nature is necessarily indefinable, even inconceivable because there is not another. *Whim*, differing from two or many, or any specificity, resembles *one* only in the sense that it can no more be thought of singly than can one be conceived as more than one. Whim cannot conceivably be one. In the *Sh'ma* the word *one* is particularly protected by the Jew against possible misapplication. So emphatic is the *Sh'ma*'s identification with one, that the word "one" is itself pronounced with an exaggerated vocal stress on the final letter, or "d", of *ehud* (one), so as not to be mistaken for the word "another" which sounds almost like *ehud*. But why all of this attention to detail in Judaism and, at least in this case, in Emerson? The answer is obvious. All of what Emerson contends and what Judaism attests, is involved in these small points. At stake is nothing less than freedom.

Emerson's substitution of Whim for *Sh'ma* inverts the Jewish meaning of freedom in favor of his own. Naturally this substitution reaches to the heart of the Jewish Idea. Emerson reverses it: that is, he reverses the Jewish meanings of oneness and freedom so that exodus, the biblical occasion of idol worship, becomes, in Emerson, the moment of man's divine new liberty. In the Bible it is of course God who is the cause of the deliverance of the Jews from bondage in Egypt. But the freedom of the Israelites is not equivalent to exodus from Egypt. Quite the contrary. The freedom of exodus until Sinai is wilderness. Particularly, it is idol worship. Exodus does not end in freedom as conquest or liberation, but in obedience at Sinai. The Israelites say we will obey even before they say they will listen to the "statutes and commandments" of God given to Moses. Exodus ends at Sinai; the promised land is promised because of it. The Israelites do not stumble upon it.

Freedom from slavery in Egypt is not freedom. More, the freedom of the desert or wilderness is exactly idol worship. In other words, freedom as exodus only, or liberation from bondage is again bondage. Idol worship would seem to be the pertinent connection between the linking of God and freedom in the Bible. "Conquest," writes Voegelin in describing Herodotus' assessment of Persian history in context of the Ionian symbol of Anaximander, "is exodus, for one must leave behind what one has in order to conquer;...this expansion of existence beyond the order of existence achieved arouses the envy of the gods."[12] The Jewish situation is certainly to be considered in this connection, with this difference: the exodus from Egypt is God's conquest, not the Jews'. This is the point that is made in the *Sh'ma* and in the First Commandment. Freedom that is only exodus, that is, idol worship, must occasion the anger of God. Do we not typically understand the episode of the Golden Calf in this context? The making of this idol so inflames the divine wrath that the entire Jewish people is brought to the brink of annihilation. It was Aaron, the chief priest, who succumbed to the people's demands for idols when they had grown weary of waiting for Moses to return from the Mountain. The effect if not the fact of Aaron's submission and surely that of the impatient Jews is the embodiment of whim. Even the calf wrought from the Egyptian earrings worn by the Israelites was a freak. "I cast" the gold into the fire, said Aaron weakly to Moses, "and there came out this calf."[13] It could have been anything. It chanced to be a calf. The point is that all idols are different and alike in that the making and worshipping of one idol is equivalent to the making and worshipping of all. Idolatry embodies the magic of eristic reasoning. It is witness to man as god, or to the attempt to transpose the many into the one. To worship one idol is to worship all of them.

The "conquest" made by the One and demonstrated to the Jews is acknowledged in the First Commandment; I am the Lord your God who brought you out of Egypt. This declaration is then a kind of definition of freedom as well as of God. No less important, it is also a declaration of common sense, of reasonable judgment regarding the facts, since it is clear the Jews did not free themselves, part the sea, or perform the other miracles and wonders of the leaving of Eygpt. In contrast, the liberty that the Jews take when Moses is gone is irrational. When they revise the *Sh'ma* subsequent to the forming of the golden calf, they proclaim, "These be your gods, O Israel, which brought you up out of the land of Egypt."[14] Logically "God" and "freedom" are still to be conceived as exodus from Egypt, but they have now been radically revised by the substitution of a palpable falsehood. The golden calf, just made, did not deliver the Jews from Egypt. More correctly, the makers of the golden calf, the Jews, did not bring themselves out of Egypt. Recall in this connection the actual crime of Nebuchadnezzar. It was the making of an idol. In this he demonstrated his ignorance that only "the most High rules in the Kingdom of man, and gives it to whomever he will." Nebuchadnezzar's punishment, his being sent to eat grass like oxen, was ended when he acknowledged this. At precisely that point his reason was restored to him. The meaning of Emerson's wish to excel in divinity is clear. Reason he considered man's, not God's, because man is free. The source of man's reason is his access to "the mind of the Creator," in particular to the reality otherwise veiled by the apeirontic aspect of being, including man's being. Access by way of reason as it is actually granted to man, that is, participation in the metaxy, is a self-denial of godhood that Emerson spurns. He calls this denial the condition of ruined man. Instead, man is to excel in divinity, to be "one with God." Man thinks God's thoughts. This is auto-revelation. In Judaism, and in the classical tradition, the source of reason is "revelation"; the mind is moved by the object.[15]

The Jewish context, Emerson well knew, is not adaptable to Emersonian ends because those ends call for the elimination of the "terrific Jewish Idea." Emerson's freedom is "wildness or a holistic" freedom as Bloom correctly perceives.[16] Like Aaron's Jews, Emerson could not wait for God's messenger to come down from the Mountain. Instead he would be "a transparent eye-ball." Thus transformed and free, "I am nothing; I see all. The currents of the Universal Being circulate through me; I am part or particle of God." (N, CW, I, 10) Finally, there shall be the "influx of the spirit" when reality will utterly vanish, leaving one free entirely. The perfect circle and all the world is the empty hole in the wheel. Emerson's is the freedom that is fulfilled, as with Aaron's Jews, in the wilderness. It pretends that the leaving of Egypt was a victory of the Jews; a war of national liberation, if one might so call it. The Jews made this mistake as well, exulting in the drowning of Egyptians in the Red Sea as if they, the Jews, not God, had parted the waters – insisting that they, or the idols, not God, "brought you out of the land of Egypt, from the house of bondage."

The elimination of the metaxy permits "the flooding of consciousness with imaginations of transfigured reality...[and thus the devaluation of] existence in the cosmos under the conditions of its structure."[17] The metaxy is unbalanced. When this happens the truth of existence is obscured. In its place is the millennial vision that is to transfigure all things. Reason and reality become the enemies of revolutionary man, to be replaced by "the one thing" which Emerson says "we seek with insatiable desire,....to forget ourselves, to be surprised out of our propriety, to lose our sempiternal memory, and to do something without knowing how or why; in short, to draw a new circle."("C", CW, II, 190)

The *contemptus mundi* that marks Emerson's Orphic vision, permitting him to delight in the "meal in the firkin" ("AS", CW, I, 67) so long as it is considered a piece of God, is ultimately a contempt of reason, thence of divinity. When Emerson's Nebuchadnezzar is freed from his bovine captivity he must become a man-god, indeed a pharaoh with dominion "such as now is beyond his dream of God." Simultaneous with Nebuchadnezzar's release from his ruined condition comes the "influx of spirit." But this is not the return to reason but the turning from it. The reward of this turning or conversion is not freedom.

Emerson's prose, as a recent observer has said, was undoubtedly more a form "of talking than writing, [more] concerned with process...[than with] meaning." His concern with the "coalition between texts and things" was also no mere "linguistic gesture."[18]

Emerson considered speech "immortal ichor...hence these throbs & heart beatings at the door of the assembly to the end, namely, that the thought may be ejaculated as Logos or Word." (JMN, IX, 72) He attempted in truth to "excel in 'Divinity'." Therefore his assertion, as from the plain of Shinar, that "the only speech will at last be Action such as Confucius describes the Speech of God" must be taken today with the utmost seriousness. (JMN, VII, 106) It is a central fact of American history.

The study we have just completed is not a biographical one. However, we may turn with profit to a biographical aspect in conclusion. Although it was Emerson's high hope that words would at last be acts in the speech of God so that a man's words should have no meaning less than being itself, the outcome was a mockery of this hope. Toward the close of a life of speaking new objects Emerson lost the power of speech; words finally had no meaning, he became aphasic. At the end of his days Emerson was a prisoner of his own perfect circle, lost in a stream of consciousness where patterns emerged no more.

Notes

1. David Brion Davis, *The Problem of Slavery in Western Culture; The Problem of Slavery in the Age of Revolution* (Ithaca, New York, 1966, 1975), II, 536–537.

2. Ibid., 536.

3. Emil Fackenheim, *Encounters Between Judaism and Modern Philosophy. A Preface to Future Jewish Thought* (New York, 1973).

4. Davis, *The Problem of Slavery*, I, 60.

5. Isaac Mendelsohn, *Slavery in the Ancient Near East* (New York, 1949), 65.

6. Maimonides, *Laws of Slaves*, V, ch. 9; halacha 8.

7. Maimonides, *Sefer Ha-Mitzvot*, trans. Charles B. Chavel (2 vols.; London, 1967), I, 247.

8. Davis, *The Problem of Slavery*, II, 534.

9. Exodus 12:12.

10. Exodus 20:2; Numbers 15:40–41.

11. Ralph L. Rusk, *The Life of Ralph Waldo Emerson* (New York, 1949), 279.

12. Eric Voegelin, *The Ecumenic Age* (Baton Rouge, 1974), 181.

13. Exodus 32:24.

14. Ibid., 32:4.

15. Aristotle, *Metaphysics*, 1072a30.

16. Harold Bloom, *Figures of Capable Imagination* (New York, 1976), 48.

17. Voegelin, *Ecumenic Age*, 234.

18. David Porter, *Emerson and Literary Change* (Cambridge, Massachusetts, 1978), 181–183, 216.

INDEX